THE *SHOOTING* SCRIPT®

MICHAEL CLAYTON

THE SHOOTING SCRIPT®

MICHAEL CLAYTON

SCREENPLAY BY TONY GILROY

FOREWORD BY
WILLIAM GOLDMAN

A Newmarket Shooting Script® Series Book
NEWMARKET PRESS • NEW YORK

FIRST EDITION

10   9   8   7   6   5   4   3   2   1

ISBN: 978-1-55704-795-3
Library of Congress Catalog-in-Publication Data available upon request.

QUANTITY PURCHASES

Companies, professional groups, clubs, and other organizations may qualify for special terms when ordering quantities
of this title. For information, write to Special Sales, Newmarket Press, 18 East 48th Street, New York, NY 10017;
call (212) 832-3575 or 1-800-669-3903; FAX (212) 832-3629; or e-mail info@newmarketpress.com.

Website: www.newmarketpress.com

Manufactured in the United States of America.

OTHER BOOKS IN THE NEWMARKET SHOOTING SCRIPT® SERIES INCLUDE:

CONTENTS

FOREWORD

BY WILLIAM GOLDMAN

Try, just *try* and stop reading the following:

> It's 2:00 a.m. in a major New York law
> firm. Ten floors of office space in the heart
> of the Sixth Avenue Canyon. Seven hours
> from now this place will be vibrating with
> the beehive energy of six hundred attorneys
> and their attendant staff, but for the moment
> it is a vast, empty, half-lit shell. A SERIES
> OF SHOTS emphasizing the size and power
> of this organization; shots that build quietly
> to the idea that somewhere here—somewhere
> in this building—there's something very
> important going on.

That is the very tense opening of *Michael Clayton* by Tony Gilroy, and as remarkable a beginning as I've come across lately.

Why do I think it's so impressive?

Two reasons. #1: The opening of a movie, any movie, is crucial. You are telling the reader—or, if you're very lucky—the viewer this: pay attention!

You don't need bombs going off, you don't need Ingrid and Bogie cooing at each other. What you need is something that tells the audience, Hey, forget about getting the damn popcorn, *this is going to be a good story.*

And I think the above opening tells us just that. We are going to a place we have never been, and something secretive is going to happen.

Reason #2 is this: the whole intro is total screenwriter's bullshit. It's what we do, and Gilroy does it as well as anybody, but think about it. All you will see is a bunch of boring offices with a bunch of boring people working some snoozy fax machines. What did I just write? That we are going someplace we have never been, and something secretive is about to happen.

But look—as screenwriters, more than anything, *we want to control your eye*. So bullshit or not, this is a successful start to a flick—no one is going to stop reading.

Or in this case, stop watching, because *Michael Clayton* is coming to a theatre near you, maybe as you turn these pages. I have seen it, and for me it's not just one of the best movies of the year. (Which may or may not be saying a whole lot, because this year so far—I am writing this in early August—is one of the most putrescent in movie history. I mean, if *Ishtar* had just been released, some critics would be having orgasms, claiming at last an Oscar-quality flick had appeared on the horizon.)

Michael Clayton—with George Clooney giving the performance of his career in the title role—is more than just a marvelous movie. It's one of the best debut directing jobs in a very long time.

Look, I am not a fan of most film directors. Any number of reasons, but mainly this: most of them suck.

But it ain't easy money at the brick factory.

And most of them whiff their first time at bat.

Why was Gilroy so solid so soon?

Total guess: because *Michael Clayton* is a thriller. Yes, its main character is a loser lawyer, yes, the amount of onscreen violence might total all of sixty seconds.

But there is a pulse beating under every frame of this mother. And you may not know this—no reason you should—but over the last years Gilroy has become—with no one in second place—the leading thriller writer in the movie world.

Do you know how hard that is?

Hang with me a second here: let's assume you were a screenwriter and you were offered a job.

Yesss!

But there were a few knotty problems to be handled.

(a) It had to be a tight, taut, rough, violent thriller.

(b) Based on a mediocre novel.

(c) That everyone had already turned down.

(d) And this tight, taut, rough, violent thriller had to have as its star—wait for it—ADAM SANDLER.

What's a mother to do?

The reason I know everybody turned down *The Bourne Identity* was because I was one of those who did. We are back around 1980 and there was a terrific opening sequence—an almost dead guy is dragged from the sea—and then it went off a cliff.

Everybody passed on the movie.

It was made into a television mini-series that not a lot of people remember. 1988. End of story.

Enter Tony Gilroy.

He takes this piece of uninspiring material and writes a movie that becomes a worldwide blockbuster.

Starring Matt Damon.

Do you know how amazing that is? I love Matt Damon, have since I first read *Good Will Hunting*. He is smart, charming, a really good writer, a marvelous, sensitive actor.

But an action star? Inconceivable, as Vizzini would say.

But they followed Gilroy's script and everyone's career went straight up. Tony wrote the second, too, *The Bourne Supremacy*, which was even more successful.

And the third one, *The Bourne Ultimatum*, which had THE MOST SUCCESSFUL OPENING IN THE HISTORY OF AUGUST! (That kind of thing matters Out There.)

If Gilroy can make Adam Sandler—oops, Matt Damon—the muscle star of his generation, having George Clooney this time around is a breeze.

Think you can do it? Good going.

I know I can't.

—August 7, 2007

Michael Clayton

by

Tony Gilroy

Final Shooting Script
2/11/06

INT. KENNER BACH & LEDEEN/VARIOUS SHOTS -- NIGHT

It's 2:00 a.m. in a major New York law firm. Ten floors
of office space in the heart of the Sixth Avenue Canyon.
Seven hours from now this place will be vibrating with the
beehive energy of six hundred attorneys and their attendant
staff, but for the moment it is a vast, empty, half-lit
shell. A SERIES OF SHOTS emphasizing the size and power of
this organization; shots that build quietly to the idea that
somewhere here -- somewhere in this building -- there's
something very important going on. MUSIC and CREDITS already
mixing with the crazed, manic, express train chatter of --

                    ARTHUR EDENS (V.O.)
          ...Michael. Dear, Michael. Nurse
          Michael. Dr. Clayton. Secret Hero.
          Keeper of the Hidden Sins. Of course
          it's you. Who else could they send?
          Who else could be trusted? Smoke on
          the horizon -- hole in the bucket --
          voices crying from Milwaukee to
          Manhattan, "Where's our hero?"
          "Where's our Cleanser Of The Hidden
          Sins?" And here you are, sleeves
          rolled up, lips sealed -- broom --
          dustbin -- bankroll at the ready!
          Fifties, is it still fifties? When
          you came to Boston, you remember?
          God, you must've had a thousand of
          them! The cash -- the smile -- the
          quiet word in the corner -- of course
          it's you, Michael, who else could it
          ever be? But Michael, please, before
          you sweep, please just hear me out --
          just try -- because it's not like
          Boston -- it's not an episode --
          relapse -- fuck up -- I'm begging
          you, Michael, make believe it's not
          just madness, because it's not just
          madness --
               (continuing, as--)

INT. LAW FIRM OFFICE/DUPLICATION CENTER -- NIGHT

A XEROX MACHINE -- cranking out high-speed copies -- ten
pages a second flashing before our eyes -- all information
a blur except for the letterhead which is constant:

KENNER, BACH & LEDEEN LLP
ATTORNEYS AT LAW

As...

>   ARTHUR EDENS (V.O.)
> -- I mean, <u>yes</u> -- okay, <u>yes</u> -- *elements
> of madness* -- the speed of madness --
> yes, the occasional, euphoric, pseudo-
> hallucinatory moments that, <u>yes</u> -- fine
> -- <u>agreed</u> -- distracting -- nostalgic --
> all of that --
>   (continuing, as--)

A HUGE EMPTY OFFICE BULLPEN. CUBICLES AND WORKSTATIONS.

>   ARTHUR EDENS (V.O.)
> -- but that's just the package --
> the plate -- think of it as a tax --
> The Mania Tax -- The Insanity Tax --
> or like advertising on TV -- it's the
> freight -- the weight -- it's the
> price of the show --

A LONG, DARK CORRIDOR. A CLEANING CREW IN THE DISTANCE.

>   ARTHUR EDENS (V.O.)
> -- just please, just hear me out,
> Michael, because I swear to you, this
> is so much, so <u>very</u> much more, than
> the ravings of some hypo-maniacal,
> bipolar attorney --

*DOCUMENT AREA. ODD THIS LATE. THREE ASSOCIATES STACKING
PAPERWORK ONTO A TROLLEY --*

>   ARTHUR EDENS (V.O.)
> -- Two weeks ago I came out of the
> building -- I'm running across Sixth
> Avenue -- there's a car waiting -- I
> have exactly thirty-eight minutes to
> get to Laguardia,and I'm dictating --
> there's this frantic associate running
> to keep up --

*A SENIOR PARTNER'S OFFICE. A SECURITY GUARD SNEAKING A
SMOKE IN THE DARK BY AN OPEN WINDOW.*

>   ARTHUR EDENS (V.O.)
> -- we're in the middle of the street --
> the light changes -- the traffic --
> unleashed -- it's coming -- <u>serious</u>
> traffic -- but there I am -- I'm
> babbling -- my mouth -- I can't stop --
> some ridiculous, involuntary part of my
> brain just keeps going -- I'm standing
> there <u>dictating</u> this trade secret,
> Motion to Suppress...

AN OFFICE PHONE. TWELVE LINES BLINKING IN THE DARK.

                    ARTHUR EDENS (V.O.)
          ...and <u>there</u>, Michael, in the middle
          of Sixth Avenue -- as I stood there
          <u>jabbering</u> -- and this poor young woman
          is screaming -- traffic speeding toward
          us -- I looked at my hands and my suit
          -- my <u>briefcase</u> -- and it came to me --
          came <u>over</u> me -- <u>through</u> me -- the
          overwhelming sensation -- the feeling --
          the <u>fact</u> -- that I was covered with
          some sort of <u>film</u> -- an oil -- an <u>ooze</u>
          -- my hair -- my face -- like a glaze --
          a coating -- and at first I thought,
          "My God, I know what this is, this is
          some sort of amniotic, embryonic fluid -
          - I'm drenched in afterbirth -- I've
          breached the chrysalis -- I've been
          reborn." --

*ASSOCIATE #1 WHEELING THAT DOCUMENT TROLLEY PAST AN EMPTY
BACK OFFICE KITCHEN.*

                    ARTHUR EDENS (V.O.)
          -- but the traffic -- this stampede --
          cars -- trucks -- the horns -- the
          screaming associate -- I'm thinking,
          "No -- <u>reset</u> -- this cannot be rebirth.
          If anything, this must some giddy
          illusion of renewal that happens in the
          final instant <u>before</u> death." --

A MAINTENANCE WORKER VACUUMING A LARGE RECEPTION STAIRCASE.

                    ARTHUR EDENS (V.O.)
          -- and then -- in the fraction of a
          moment it took for that idea to form --
          I realized <u>all</u> of that was wrong,
          because I looked back at the building
          and had the most stunning moment of
          clarity...

*THE WORD PROCESSING DEPARTMENT. TWENTY PEOPLE -- ACTORS,
DANCERS, ARTISTS, INSOMNIACS -- THE GRAVEYARD SHIFT
HAMMERING OUT OVERNIGHT LEGAL PAPERWORK.*

                    ARTHUR EDENS (V.O.)
          ...I realized, Michael, at that moment,
          that I had emerged -- as I have done
          nearly every day for the past twenty-
          eight years of my life -- <u>not</u> through
          doors of Kenner, Bach & Ledeen --

*RECEPTION LOBBY. ASSOCIATE #1 WHEELING THE TROLLEY OFF
THE ELEVATOR.*

> ARTHUR EDENS (V.O.)
> -- <u>not</u> through the portals of our huge
> and powerful law firm, but rather from
> the asshole of an organism whose sole
> function is to excrete the poison --
> the ammo -- the <u>defoliant</u> -- necessary
> for even larger and more dangerous
> organisms to destroy the miracle of
> humanity --

*ANOTHER EMPTY HALLWAY. A BANQUET TABLE LITTERED WITH THE
PICKED-OVER REMNANTS OF AN ALL-NIGHT CATERED FEED.*

> ARTHUR EDENS (V.O.)
> -- and that I have been coated with
> this patina of shit for the better part
> of my life and that the stink and stain
> might in all likelihood take the rest
> of my days to undo --

*AND NOW -- WIDER TO FIND -- ASSOCIATE #1 WHEELING THE
TROLLEY TOWARD BIG DOORS AT THE END OF THE HALL --*

> ARTHUR EDEN'S (V.O.)
> -- and do you know what I did next?
> I took a deep, cleansing breath.
> I set that notion aside. I tabled it.
> I said to myself, "As clear as this may
> be -- as <u>potent</u> as this may feel -- as
> true a thing as I believe I have
> witnessed here -- I must wait. It must
> stand the test of time."

*AN ATTORNEY HUDDLED OVER HIS MOBILE PHONE, SEEING THE KID
COMING, HELPING HIM BY OPENING THE DOORS, as --*

> ARTHUR EDENS (V.O.)
> And, Michael, the time is now.

<u>INT.   LAW FIRM CONFERENCE ROOM -- NIGHT</u>

The big room. Bright. <u>Teeming</u>. FORTY PEOPLE jamming an
all-night deadline: ATTORNEYS -- PARTNERS AND ASSOCIATES --
PARALEGALS -- ASSISTANTS -- ACCOUNTANTS -- working groups
bunkered around a huge table <u>covered</u> with paperwork and
laptops and coffee mugs. Several document "villages" piled
around the room. The credits have wrapped. Arthur Edens has
stopped talking. And if there's music, that's stopped too.
<u>We're live</u>.

BARRY GRISSOM coming around the table. He's maybe fifty.
A killer New York lawyer in his prime. Litigator. Senior
partner. Always wrapped a little tight and this moment is
no exception -- slowing now and...

>   BARRY
>   (kneeling, whispering)
>   I've got that cunt from the Wall Street
>   Journal on line eight. I told her you
>   were in Bermuda, but I'd try to patch
>   you in...

MARTY BACH looks up from his papers. He's seventy. It's
his name on the door. Big power. Sweet eyes. A thousand
neckties. A velvet switchblade.

>   MARTY
>   (punching up line eight)
>   Marty Bach. How can I help you?

>   REPORTER (PHONE/OVER)
>   "Marty, hi, it's Bridget Klein. Look,
>   we're going with a story tomorrow about
>   a settlement in the U/North defoliant
>   case. You want to comment?"

>   MARTY
>   The case you're referring to, is now,
>   as it has been for the past six years,
>   pending and unresolved. Until our
>   client has their day in court or the
>   plaintiffs come to their senses and
>   drop the suit, I'll have nothing of
>   value to tell you.

BARRY kneeling there, hanging on every word --

>   REPORTER (PHONE/OVER)
>   "Come on, Marty, Barry's telling me
>   you're off at some conference. I know
>   for a fact you're in the office right
>   now with like six hundred people trying
>   to push this thing through."

>   MARTY
>   Here's what I know: your deadline was
>   twenty minutes ago, so either you're
>   fishing for a story or trying to get
>   out of writing a retraction. In either
>   case, I wish you well...best of luck...
>   (as he hangs up--)
>   ...sweet dreams.

                         BARRY
          So?

                         MARTY
                    (scanning the room)
          Where the fuck is Karen Crowder?

INT. LAW FIRM LADIES ROOM -- NIGHT

A CORPORATE LOGO -- embossed on a high-quality, Kevlar,
travel tote:

u/north

"we grow your world together"

THE U/NORTH BAG on a shelf above a row of sinks. Water
running. But no one there. Stalls in the mirror and --

INT. LADIES ROOM STALL -- NIGHT

KAREN CROWDER sitting fully dressed on the john. She is
Senior In-House Counsel for the largest agricultural/chemical
supply manufacturer on the planet. She is hiding here. She
is trying to fight off a panic attack using a breathing
exercise she read about in an airline magazine. As we hear:

                    ARTHUR EDENS (V.O.)
               ...even this, Michael -- even now --
               that you're here -- there's a reason,
               a reason it's you -- every reason --
               surely you can sense that -- how it
               pulls together -- how it gathers --
               Nurse Michael -- Secret Hero -- Keeper
               of the Hidden Sins -- tell me you can
               see that, Michael, for God's sake...

INT. CHINATOWN CARD ROOM -- NIGHT

MICHAEL CLAYTON'S FACE -- A PHOTOGRAPH laminated onto a
Kenner, Bach & Ledeen ID card -- FILLS OUR FRAME. It's a
man's face. Son of a second-generation cop's face. Father
of a ten-year-old boy's face. A face women like more than
they know why. The good soldier's face. THE ID CARD just
one of several objects sitting at the bottom of a shitty
plastic basket. Also here: one roll of breath mints, two
mobile phones, business cards, too many keys on a Mercedes
security pendant keychain, and one heavy-duty steel Rolex.

PULL BACK TO REVEAL

THREE OTHER BASKETS ON THE TABLE. Three other sets of
personal objects. A SMALL HOLSTERED GUN in one of the
collections. A stack of empty baskets to the side.

E *

WE'RE IN

A CHINATOWN CASINO. A basement hideaway on a dead night.
TWO BORED CHINESE BOUNCERS sitting with the plastic baskets
beside a walk-through metal detector. Only one of the room's
ten tables is lit tonight. In the background, a Cantonese
Announcer calling the first race at Happy Valley and --

MICHAEL CLAYTON glancing at his four hole cards. Four up
cards in the middle of the table. The game is Pot Limit
Omaha and the eyes are weary tonight.

                    MICHAEL
          Check.

THE DEALER is Chinese and all business -- looking to --

                    PLAYER #2
               (Dominican dude)
          I go like that. Check.

PLAYER #3 has a bad toupee and a plumber's flashroll --

                    PLAYER #3/PLUMBER
               (peeling off twenties)
          Half the pot. Two hundred.

PLAYER #4, a Chinese landlord -- already pushing his cards
away -- he's folding --

                    DEALER
               (back to Michael)
          Two hundred to you.

MICHAEL shakes his head. He's out. PLAYER #2 right behind
him. THE DEALER starts gathering cards for the next hand.

                    PLUMBER
          You don't remember me, huh?
               (to Michael as he rakes
               in the pot--)
          We played a couple times that lamp
          place. On Bowery. That guy's
          showroom. All the lamps and shit?

                    MICHAEL
          Galaxy.

                    PLUMBER
          That's it. You had a restaurant you
          opened, right? On Franklin? Cause
          my old partner bid that job, the
          plumbing. You don't remember me?

                    MICHAEL
          I remember.

                    PLUMBER
          I lost a lot of weight since then.

                    MICHAEL
          You bought some hair.

                    PLUMBER
          Yeah, with your money.

MICHAEL just posts his blind. Tune him out.

                    PLUMBER
          So your bar, what happened? Just had
          to be in show biz, right?

                    PLAYER #2
          Shit, man...
               (getting cranky)
          I want to listen to Larry King, I'll go
          home and put the fucking TV on.

                    PLUMBER
               (just ignoring him)
          Cause that was a good location.

                    MICHAEL
          Yeah, that's what my partner kept
          telling me.

Cards coming out as we --

ANGLE ON

THE BASKET WITH MICHAEL'S STUFF. THE PAGER starts vibrating.
A moment later, THE CELL PHONE starts ringing and --

INT. CHINATOWN FREIGHT ELEVATOR -- NIGHT

Ascending. MICHAEL leaving in a hurry. Strapping on his
Rolex, trying to read the pager and --

EXT. DOYERS ST. -- NIGHT

Late. Cold. Quiet. MICHAEL coming up the street, juggling
a remote security pendant and A CELL PHONE --

                    MICHAEL (OS)
          -- is he drunk?

                    MALE VOICE (PHONE)
                (nervous, hyper)
          "-- no, that's the first thing I asked
          him -- no, he's sober --"

                    MICHAEL
          -- tell him to stay off the phone --

                    MALE VOICE (PHONE)
          "-- so, Michael, I mean, you're on it
          now, right? Because this guy, he's a
          huge client -- this is half my book,
          this guy, okay?"

                    MICHAEL
          I'm walking to my car.

                    MALE VOICE (PHONE)
          "Let me give you my number in Bermuda,
          I gotta call him right back and let him
          know you're on the way."

A BLACK MERCEDES comes alive -- lights flaring as the alarm
disables and --

EXT. WEST SIDE HIGHWAY -- NIGHT

THE MERCEDES speeding North.

INT. THE MERCEDES -- NIGHT (CONT)

MICHAEL trying to drive and mess with the GPS UNIT on his
dashboard. Something's wrong with it. He's tapping on it
and THE SCREEN is flickering on and off -- finally, fuck it
-- he slaps the GPS away -- steps on the gas and --

EXT. WEST SIDE HIGHWAY -- NIGHT (CONT)

THE MERCEDES racing toward the George Washington bridge.

EXT. WESTCHESTER MANSION -- NIGHT

THE MERCEDES pulling up the long dark driveway.

INT. MANSION GARAGE -- NIGHT

THE DAMAGED FRONT BODY PANEL OF A MERCEDES. Dented in.
MICHAEL'S HAND -- his pen -- examining the freshly-chipped
paint, until --

MICHAEL stands. We see him now. The Mercedes just one of
half-a-dozen luxury vehicles lined up here in this bright
oversized garage.

INT. MANSION KITCHEN -- NIGHT

Mega kitchen. The scale and taste of real wealth.

                    MR. GREER
               (pacing)
          What they did, you see, they changed
          the grade there. They widened the
          street, I'm sure someone told them
          they were making an improvement...

MICHAEL on a stool at the island. MRS. GREER standing by
herself. Nightgown pulled tight. Her second tumbler of
Scotch.

                    MR. GREER
          But now, you see, when it rains?
          With this new angle, and they put
          these new these sodium lamps -- it's
          blinding, that turn there. Just
          blinding.

                    MICHAEL
          They'll have to take a look at that.

                    MR. GREER
          And this, it's not just tonight.
          I've been saying this for years.
               (to his wife)
          How many times have we talked about
          that corner? Gen?

MRS. GREER silent. Numb.

                    MICHAEL
          Mr. Greer, we don't have a great deal
          of time to work with here.

MR. GREER's anxiety sharpening. Arrogance under siege.

                    MR. GREER
          So the circumstances, road conditions,
          none of this holds any interest for
          you?

                    MICHAEL
          What interests me right now is finding
          the strongest criminal attorney that
          can get here in the next fifteen
          minutes.

                    MR. GREER
               (bristling)
          Well, that sounds ominous...

                    MICHAEL
          We have some good relationships up
          here in Westchester.

                    MR. GREER
          So what are you? You're not a lawyer?

                    MICHAEL
          Not the kind you need.

                    MR. GREER
          What kind is that?

                    MICHAEL
          You need a trial lawyer. Someone
          to see this all the way through.
          That's not what I do.

There it is. And MR. GREER doesn't like it one bit.

                    MR. GREER
          I think we're gonna need to pull Walter
          back in on this.
               (like it's some kind of
                business meeting)
          I want to get him back on the phone,
          get him into the mix. Because, I'll
          be frank, I'm not sure I like the way
          this is going.

                    MICHAEL
          Sir...
               (cut the crap)
          We don't have time for Walter.
          Your options here, they're gonna get
          smaller very quickly.

                    MR. GREER
          What options? I'm not hearing any
          options.

                    MICHAEL
          I'm suggesting you go local. I'm
          telling you there's several people up
          here I like for this.

                    MR. GREER
          And that's it? That's what you've got?
               (to his wife)
          You believe this?
                              (MORE)

                         MR. GREER (cont'd)
                    (incredulous)
          I've been a client at Kenner, Bach
          for twelve years! You think I pay
          that retainer every month for a place
          at the back of the line?

                         MICHAEL
          Mr. Greer, you left the scene of an
          accident on a slow weeknight, six
          miles from the State Police barracks.
          Believe me, if there's a line, you're
          right up front.

                         MR. GREER
          I can get a lawyer any time I want!
          You think I need you for that? You
          think we're sitting here forty-five
          minutes waiting for a goddam <u>referral</u>?

                         MICHAEL
          Look, I don't know what Walter promised
          you, but whatever it w--

                         MR. GREER
          "Miracle Worker."
                    (cutting him cold)
          That's a direct quote. That's Walter
          twenty minutes ago, okay? "Hang tight,
          I'm sending you a miracle worker!"

                         MICHAEL
          Well, he misspoke.

                         MR. GREER
          About what? That you're the firm's
          fixer? Or that you're any good at it?

                         MRS. GREER
          <u>Elliot</u>...

                         MR. GREER
          This guy was running in the street!
                    (losing it)
          You add the lights -- the rain --
          the angle -- what kind of person's
          out running in the street in the rain
          at midnight? Answer me th--
                    (stopping instantly, as--)

GLASS SHATTERS! -- MRS. GREER just hurled her highball into
the sink. Staring at her husband. Silence, until --

                        MR. GREER
            What if someone had stolen the car?
            Happens all the time.
                    (dead air)
            Hypothetically...

This awful pause. MICHAEL wielding the silence like a club.

                        MICHAEL
            Cops like hit and run cases. They
            work them hard and they clear them
            fast. Right now, there's a BCI unit
            picking paint chips off a guardrail.
            Tomorrow morning they're gonna be
            looking for the owner of a custom-
            color, hand-rubbed, green Mercedes SL
            500. This guy you hit, if he got a
            look at the plate, it won't even take
            that long.

Like that -- THE PHONE RINGS -- harsh -- sudden --

                        MRS. GREER
            ...omigod...

                        MICHAEL
                    (ignoring the phone)
            There's no play here. There's no
            angle. There's no champagne room.
            And I'm not a miracle worker, I'm a
            janitor. So the math on this is
            simple: the smaller the mess, the
            easier it is for me to clean up.

THE PHONE STILL RINGING and --

                        MR. GREER
                    (small now)
            It's the police, isn't it?

                        MICHAEL
            No. They don't call.
                    (calmly picking up--)
            Hello?
                    (beat)
            Jerry. Hey, it's Michael...
                    (pause)
            Yeah, sorry. I'm in the neighborhood.
            You got a pen?

MICHAEL on hold. Silence now. MR. AND MRS. GREER parked
like glaciers. Broken glass in the sink.

EXT. WESTCHESTER MANSION DRIVEWAY -- NIGHT

One hour later. MICHAEL leaning on the MERCEDES, munching
on a loaf of stale French bread. Looking over, as JERRY
DANTE, local criminal attorney, comes out of the house --

                    JERRY
          He's changing his shirt...
               (as he arrives)
          I talked to my guy at the State Police
          barracks. Better we go over there and
          surrender and they can tell the town
          cops to kiss off. This kid he hit,
          he's a waiter at one of those clubs
          along the strip there. He's stable.
          I guess they're putting some pins in
          his hip. Good news is he got busted
          selling pot last year, so we got
          something to work with anyway.

                    MICHAEL
          You don't need me for this, right?

                    JERRY
          Couldn't hurt.

                    MICHAEL
          I'll have somebody call you.

JERRY nods. Okay. But lingering a moment, because --

                    JERRY
          So, Michael, look, I was thinking of
          you last week. My cousin Frank, from
          Brooklyn Kings, right? He's out in
          Nassau now. They got an opening on
          the probate bench. He's kind of going
          for it.

                    MICHAEL
          That's a tough crowd.

                    JERRY
          No shit. Can I have him call you?

                    MICHAEL
          Sure.

                    JERRY
          And don't worry about this...
               (re: Mr. Greer)
          I'll put my back into it.

MICHAEL nods. Heading for the car and --

EXT.   MANSION DRIVEWAY/COUNTRY ROAD -- NIGHT

THE MERCEDES speeding away from the house --

INT.   THE MERCEDES -- NIGHT

MICHAEL driving. Escaping. Running from more than Mr. Greer
and Jerry Dante. More than just a bad night boiling behind
his eyes. Driving hard and wild. Turning suddenly and --

EXT.   WESTCHESTER COUNTRY ROAD -- NIGHT

THE MERCEDES racing along.

INT.   THE MERCEDES -- NIGHT/PRE-DAWN

MICHAEL -- turning again -- aimless -- windows open --
cold air whipping through -- braking suddenly -- impulsive
-- turning -- suddenly -- faster now and --

EXT.   NEW COUNTRY ROAD -- PRE-DAWN

First light. A smaller road. THE MERCEDES speeding past
large estates tucked back in the fog and deep woods.

EXT.   THE FIELD -- DAWN

A HUGE OPEN PASTURE. Surrounded by forest. The sun just
starting to rise. Cold mist hanging over the whole valley.
Nothing but gray and green. Stark. Perfect.

THE MERCEDES speeding toward us -- climbing around the turn --
eating up the valley road that runs along the pasture -- but
suddenly the car is slowing -- braking hard and --

INT.   THE MERCEDES -- DAWN

MICHAEL pulling to a stop. Staring out the window.

EXT.   THE FIELD -- DAWN

MICHAEL getting out of the car. Standing there.

THREE HORSES poised at the crest of the pasture. Hanging
there in the fog like ghosts.

MICHAEL jumping the fence. Walking slowly into the field.
Behind him, the MERCEDES with the engine running.

THE HORSES aware of him now. Watching him come.

MICHAEL'S FACE as he walks. And later on we'll understand
all the forces roiling inside him, but for the moment, the
simplest thing to say is that this is a man who needs more

than anything to see one pure, natural thing, and by some miracle has found his way to this place. The wet grass and cold air and no coat -- none of it makes any difference to him right now -- he's a pilgrim stumbling into the cathedral.

And he stops. Just standing there. Empty. Open. Lost.

Nothing but the field and the fog and the woods beyond.

THE HORSES staring at him.

MICHAEL staring back. And just like that...

<u>THE MERCEDES EXPLODES!</u>

THE HORSES already running before MICHAEL can turn back -- pieces of the car that have been blown into the sky still raining down before he's fully grasped what's happening --

MICHAEL simply shocked. Senseless. Standing there frozen. Stunned. *What just happened?* The car -- his car -- is <u>gone</u> -- just like that. MICHAEL looks around. Looks back. He should be dead. He is not.

When THE GAS TANK EXPLODES!

And suddenly it's clear. All that staggered chaos in Michael's eyes suddenly replaced with steel. He should be dead. He is not.

And now he's walking. <u>Toward</u> the car.

Walking faster. Determined. And suddenly he's running -- running *toward* the fire. Faster and faster, as we...

DISSOLVE TO

INT. HENRY CLAYTON'S BEDROOM -- DAY

A COMPUTER MONITOR. A screen saver. Dragon-Slaying Wizards, Orcs, Nordic Elves, Samurai Gnomes -- all spinning across the monitor in perpetual slow motion. And every few seconds these words appear:

REALM & CONQUEST

WIDER TO REVEAL

The small room of a typical pre-war West End apartment. Loft bed. Parquet floor. Paint-chipped radiator. All of this subsidiary, however to the room's overwhelming

decorative theme: <u>Fantasy</u>. Books, games, posters, models --
hundreds of mythical lands, creatures, weapons and journeys
are stacked, pinned, piled and catalogued everywhere.

FOUR DAYS EARLIER

HENRY CLAYTON is ten -- small for ten -- all bones and
intelligence. He's hustling around, stuffing things into
his already bulging backpack -- rushing off, taking us with
him into --

INT. WEST END HALLWAY/KITCHEN -- DAY

HENRY scrambling through a hallway clogged with books and
bookshelves -- a clutter of intellectual/domestic funk --
bringing us quickly to the kitchen and IVY, Michael's ex-
wife. She is 38. Her youthful beauty perhaps a bit too
delicate for life's perpetual harassments. GERALD was Ivy's
doctoral history professor, now he's her second husband.
He's feeding SOPHIA, their eighteen-month old daughter.

> HENRY
> (blowing through--)
> Is my other deck in here?

> IVY
> Did you eat?

> HENRY
> (scrounging around)
> Dad's down there waiting already.

> GERALD
> There were cards in our bathroom.

> HENRY
> (Ivy staring at him)
> <u>Yes</u>. I had a waffle.

> IVY
> Since we're out of waffles I don't
> see how that's possible.

> HENRY
> (rushing off)
> It's a miracle.

IVY about to fire back. GERALD waving her off. Let it go.
Feed the baby. Save your strength.

EXT. WEST END AVENUE - DAY

MICHAEL in the Mercedes stopped at the corner. The good
suit and tie.

>   MICHAEL
>   (as he sees him--)
>   Henry!

EXT. BROADWAY/UPPER WEST SIDE -- DAY

THE MERCEDES driving through morning traffic, as we hear --

>   HENRY (V.O.)
>   ...so no one's even sure exactly
>   where they are because there's no
>   border or landmarks or anything...

INT. THE MERCEDES -- DAY (CONT)

MICHAEL driving. HENRY shotgun.

>   HENRY
>   ...and the town, it's not even a
>   town, really, it's just like this camp
>   where these people have gathered to
>   hide, right? All these deserters and
>   guys that got cut off from their
>   armies, all these people that were
>   hiding in the woods and trying to stay
>   alive, this is where they all came.
>   There's Thieves, Gray Mages, Unbidden
>   Warriors, Dark Avians, Riverwynders,
>   Sappers -- there's like fifteen kinds
>   of characters, okay?

>   MICHAEL
>   Okay.

MICHAEL fighting distraction. HENRY so eager and serious.

>   HENRY
>   So basically you have all these
>   characters who don't know each other
>   and they don't know why they're here
>   and nobody has any alliances, okay?
>   Whatever alliances you had before are
>   gone. You can't even say who you are,
>   because you don't know, maybe the
>   person you're talking to, maybe they
>   were like your mortal enemy in the
>   wars. So it's just completely like
>   everybody for themselves.

                    MICHAEL
          Sounds familiar.

                    HENRY
          It's really good. I'm serious.
          You should really read it.

                    MICHAEL
          Right. And by the time I finish it
          you're gonna be onto something else.

                    HENRY
          How much you want to bet?

                    MICHAEL
          I don't know. How much you got?

MICHAEL glances over. The boy just aching with sweetness.

                    HENRY ———————————————————————————— SON
          It's not just the deck and legend
          books, it's a massive player online
          RPG and they're gonna do gaming
          figures too. They worked on this for
          like six years.

But they're here. MICHAEL to the curb behind school vans.

                    MICHAEL
          Bus pass?

                    HENRY
          It's in my locker.
              (pissed)
          You're not even gonna look at it,
          are you?

                    MICHAEL
          What? The book? Bring it Saturday.

                    HENRY
          I did already. I left it in your
          kitchen. It's got a red cover.

                    MICHAEL
          Go.
              (snagging a quick kiss)
          Go on. Teach these people something.

HENRY getting out of the car. MICHAEL watching his son lug
his backpack down the sidewalk and into the school. MICHAEL
holding a smile, ready with a final wave goodbye. And then
the boy is gone and the mask comes down. Checking his watch
-- he's late and tense and dropping the car into gear, as --

EXT. "TIM'S" -- DAY

A restaurant/bar near Foley Square. TIM'S was a sweet-
looking, pubbish tavern that's gone out of business.
Several vans double-parked outside as we hear --

                    AUCTIONEER (V.O.)
          ...lot 37, two Fryolater six gallon
          units. They're new, they're clean,
          let's start five hundred the pair...

INT. "TIM'S" KITCHEN -- DAY

FIFTEEN BUYERS bunched like starlings around the AUCTIONEER.
Men with clipboards. Equipment all tagged and stacked and
ready to roll.

                    AUCTIONEER
          ...five hundred, I've got five --
          five-fifty. Six. This is two units,
          folks. Six, I see six-fifty. Seven...

INT. "TIM'S" BAR/DINING ROOM -- DAY

Dark. Stripped down. Stools, blenders, cash registers --
everything stacked and tagged. MICHAEL alone at a table.
Sounds of the carcass being picked over in the BG. GABE
ZABEL, loanshark, enters from the kitchen.

                    ZABEL
          He says you're still gonna be short.

                    MICHAEL
          How short?

                    ZABEL
          Sixty. Plus the points. Seventy-five
          thousand.

A body blow. MICHAEL trying to hide the impact.

                    MICHAEL
          That's liquor and everything?

                    ZABEL
          What'd you think it was gonna be?

                    MICHAEL
          I don't know. Less. Thirty. Twenty.
               (the Auctioneer bleating
                away in the BG--)
          He's taking fifteen hundred on a
          refrigerator I paid four grand for.

                    ZABEL
          Make a bid.

MICHAEL nods. Suck it up. Be a man.

                    ZABEL
          You don't have this seventy-five?

                    MICHAEL
          Just laying around? No.

                    ZABEL
          Where's your brother?

                    MICHAEL
          Forget that.

                    ZABEL
          Michael, look, you want to front
          this, that's up to you, but Timmy's   BROTHER
          name stays in the book until we're
          clear.
               (gentle but firm)
          If I know where he is, I don't have
          to keep asking.

                    MICHAEL
          He's upstate. His wife took him
          back. He's living in his in-laws
          basement.

                    ZABEL
          He's gotta have something.

                    MICHAEL
          Sure. He's got the two kids with   X
          her. He's got Jennifer, the coke-
          dealing waitress he knocked up --
          four Michelin snow tires he boosted
          from my sister's garage...
               (a fuck-it smile)
          Make him an offer.

ZABEL nods. His version of sympathy.

                    ZABEL
          I had a wife was a drunk. Beautiful
          girl. Young girl. But live like that?
          Even they do a program. I think she
          did once two years. It's like you're
          strapped to a bomb.

                    MICHAEL
          Timmy was sober six years.

> ZABEL
> That's what I'm saying. They slip?
> Forget it. They don't give a shit,
> they're stoned. It's everybody else
> who's got a problem.

Enough with this. They both have places to be.

> MICHAEL
> What's my time frame here?

> ZABEL
> For you? I don't know. I didn't
> think it was gonna be a problem.
>   (Michael's silence says
>   it is)
> I'll ask.

MICHAEL nods. THE AUCTIONEER still at it, as --

INT. LAW FIRM BUILDING LOBBY -- DAY

MICHAEL'S ID CARD swiping the scanner. KENNER, BACH & LEDEEN
LOGO by the elevator bank and --

INT. ELEVATOR BANK/ELEVATOR -- DAY

MICHAEL making it as the doors close. Three lawyers in here.
Dominant power is JEFF GAFFNEY. Big blowhard partner.

> GAFFNEY
> Hey, Miguel, how's it going?

> MICHAEL
> Great, Jeff, how's it with you?

Both men instantly into a superficial, glad-hand familiarity.

> GAFFNEY
> You know Brini...

> MICHAEL
> Sure.

BRINI GLASS nods hello. She's a young polished, go-getter.
The guy standing beside her a chilly, forty year-old Brit --

> GAFFNEY
> This is Paul Julian. Paul's visiting
> us from the UK...

> MICHAEL
> How you doing? Michael Clayton.

PAUL JULIAN with a quick hello. Handshake. The usual crap.

> GAFFNEY
> Michael's the guy who actually knows
> everything that's really going on here.
> (with a smile)
> He won't tell you, but he knows.

> MICHAEL
> Which is what the guys who <u>really</u>
> know what's going on always say to
> cover their tracks.
> (THE DOORS OPEN, stepping
> off as--)
> Take it easy, Jeff. Brini.

ELEVATOR DOORS CLOSE. MICHAEL, alone, drops the punchline
smile. Heading toward his office as we begin to hear --

> MICHAEL (V.O./PHONE)
> ...look, Del, I don't know how hard
> to press here. You're gonna have to
> let me know how brave he wants to be.

> DEL (V.O./PHONE)
> Well, I'm not sure how brave he <u>can</u> be
> right now. We just got a confirmation
> hearing scheduled for the end of the
> month.
> (continuing, as--)

INT. MICHAEL'S OFFICE/TIME CUTS -- DAY

A large corner twenty stories high. Midtown looming through
windows. Probably the best office on this floor. But it's
not a partner's floor. More comfortable than flashy. More
clubhouse than a place to bring clients. WALLS COVERED WITH
PHOTOGRAPHS AND MEMORABILIA. A cluttered mix of banquet
handshake pics and framed family snapshots. Two decades of
testimonial horseshit and tribal gatherings. MICHAEL pacing
and THE CAMERA WANDERING as --

> MICHAEL/PHONE
> Any chance she knows that?

> DEL/PHONE
> It was in the paper. Who knows?
> Maybe she got someone to read it to
> her.
> (incredulous)
> She called his wife. She's calling
> his house. It's a nightmare.

                    MICHAEL/PHONE
          My guess is that she's gonna want to
          hang onto this condo.

                    DEL/PHONE
          That's insane.

                    MICHAEL/PHONE
          What can I tell you? Don't piss off
          a motivated stripper.
               (wrap it up)
          Look, find out his pain threshold
          and get back to me. I'll take it from
          there. Or have him call me...

                    DEL/PHONE
          I hear you. Lemme get into it.
               (click, and--)

                    MICHAEL
               (hanging up, calling back
               out the door--)
          Where are we with Marty?

                    PAM
               (calling back)
          We left word.

TIME CUT

Later. New call. MICHAEL pacing. Speakerphone now.

                    MICHAEL/PHONE
          How old's the kid?

                    WENDY/PHONE
          He's not a kid. He's twenty-two.

                    MICHAEL/PHONE
          This is Miami?

                    WENDY/PHONE
          Key Biscayne.

                    MICHAEL/PHONE
          They charged him?

                    WENDY/PHONE
          Reckless Endangerment. My client,
          I think really what they want, they
          want a reality check on the attorney
          down there. Wayne said you had some
          connections in the area...

                    MICHAEL/PHONE
          Yup. Lemme just grab a pen...

TIME CUT

Later. New call. MICHAEL still on speakerphone.

                    RANDALL/PHONE
          What're you trying to do, Michael?
          Get me to kill the story?

                    MICHAEL/PHONE
          Randy, please... I'm saying let
          somebody else write it.

                    RANDALL/PHONE
          Why would I do that?

                    MICHAEL/PHONE
          Love? Decency? Fear? Want me to
          keep going?

                    RANDALL/PHONE
          C'mon, man...

                    MICHAEL/PHONE
                (pulling it off speaker)
          You know what story I keep waiting
          to read? The one about the business
          reporter who's sick of watching
          everyone else get rich.

Silence. Tone shift. MICHAEL waiting.

                    RANDALL/PHONE
          This is breaking news, or something
          you're just spitballing?

                    MICHAEL
          The Beverly Fund's looking for a new
          Director Of Communications. I gave
          them your name, I hope you don't mind.

TIME CUT

Later. New call. MICHAEL by the window --

                    MICHAEL/PHONE
          -- if she calls INS directly she's
          gonna get nowhere --

                    EVAN/PHONE
          -- even with the appointment? --

                    MICHAEL/PHONE
-- it's retail, Evan, it's like DMV
over there, unless they get a call from
a District Supervisor nobody moves --

                    EVAN/PHONE
-- but your guy can do that? --

                    MICHAEL/PHONE
-- he's a former Commissioner --

                    EVAN/PHONE
-- and none of this comes back to
me, right? Cause that doesn't do
anybody any good.

                    MICHAEL/PHONE
No, I'd be the one doing the asking.

                    EVAN/PHONE
Can you hang on a minute?

                    MICHAEL
Sure.
        (on hold now, glancing
         back because--)
PAM, his assistant, is in the doorway.

                    PAM
Are we merging?

                    MICHAEL
What?

                    PAM
Marty Bach's in London. First they
said he was in Atlanta, then Lara
said he was in the building, so I
called back up -- I know you want this
meeting -- now she tells me the truth,
he's really in London.
        (quiet, nervous)
Are we merging? Because that's what
everyone's saying. All these Brits.
That this time it's for real.

                    MICHAEL
Like I would know.
        (she's staring like,
         "yes, you would."--)
I don't know.

A PHONE starts ringing now from behind her --

                    PAM
          Even if we are, even if they merged,
          it wouldn't effect you, right?

                    MICHAEL
          Pam, your phone is ringing.

She steps out to answer. MICHAEL alone again. Still standing
there. Still absorbing this morning's shrapnel, as --

EXT. OMAHA NEBRASKA -- DAY

Cold morning. Stark windblown flatness. A highway on-ramp
in the foreground tells us where we are.

EXT. OMAHA RIVERFRONT TOWNHOUSES -- DAY

Modern, tidy, downtown Omaha living. As we hear:

                    KAREN (V.O.)
          At the moment, U/North currently has
          seventy thousand employees working in
          sixty-two countries around the world...
              (continuing, as we--)

INT. KAREN'S OMAHA HOME/BATHROOM -- DAY

KAREN CROWDER alone at the mirror. Fresh from the shower --

                    KAREN
          ...around the planet...sixty-two
          countries around the planet.
              (trying it again)
          At work in more than sixty countries
          around the globe.

INT. U/NORTH OMAHA CONFERENCE ROOM -- DAY

Later that morning. KAREN and her boss, DON JEFFRIES, a 60-
year-old Corporate titan, on one side of the table. Facing
them, A SMALL VIDEO CREW: CAMERAMAN, SOUND, and INTERVIEWER.
The filming part of some in-house promotional puffery --

                    KAREN
          ...right now we've got seventy-five
          thousand employees in over sixty
          countries around the planet.

INT.   KAREN'S OMAHA HOME/BATHROOM -- DAY

Twelve minutes later. Make-up at the mirror --

                KAREN
    ...so the volume...the <u>quantity</u> of
    legal issues is just overwhelming...
        (reset)
    ...just enormous.
        (trying it folksy)
    You can imagine, the volume of legal
    issues...it's just enormous...it's...

INT.   U/NORTH OMAHA CONFERENCE ROOM -- DAY

Video camera rolling and --

                KAREN
    ...it's quite substantial. As general
    counsel, what I do -- our in-house
    department -- we analyze the dimensions
    of the problem or the opportunity, we
    determine the jurisdiction, and we
    farm our business to the firms and
    talent we think can help us the most.

INT.   KAREN'S OMAHA HOME/DESK AREA -- DAY

KAREN glancing at a list of questions --

                KAREN
    Balance?
        (smiling for the imaginary
         camera--)
    I think everyone has to find their
    own mix. I like work. I enjoy my job.
        (try again)
    I find I feel most alive when I'm...
        (fuck)
    I realized a long time ago, that...
        (hating this, and--)

INT.   U/NORTH OMAHA CONFERENCE ROOM -- DAY

              INTERVIEWER
    So how do you keep a balance between
    work and life?

INT.   KAREN'S OMAHA HOME/BEDROOM

KAREN pulling on her stockings and --

                         KAREN
          Balance?
                    (trying to pretend the
                    question surprises her--)
          Honestly? I think all this concern
          about "balance" actually creates more
          stress than...

INT.   U/NORTH OMAHA CONFERENCE ROOM -- DAY

                         KAREN
          ...your priorities change, you make
          new plans. But my goal -- right now,
          today -- is to be the second best
          General Counsel this company has ever
          seen.

DON JEFFRIES, THE INTERVIEWER, everyone smiling at this --

                         KAREN
          Don brought me in here twelve years
          ago...
                    (big smile for Don)
          Trusted me. Mentored me.

INT. KAREN'S OMAHA HOME/KITCHEN -- DAY

                         KAREN
                    (having a lonely egg)
          ...and when Don moved up to the
          boardroom, I never really thought
          I'd have the opportunity to move into
          his place...
                    (reset)
          ...his position...his office...his...

INT. U/NORTH OMAHA CONFERENCE ROOM -- DAY

                         KAREN
          ...because if you're ultimately not
          comfortable with the responsibility,
          you're in the wrong place. It's your
          department. It's your ability to make
          tough decisions in real time and--
                    (stopping because--)

A SECRETARY has nervously entered the room --

                         DON JEFFRIES
          We're in the middle of an interview...

                         SECRETARY
          They said it was urgent.

INT. BARRY GRISSOM'S OFFICE -- DAY

New York power office. BARRY GRISSOM -- the senior partner
we met in the opening scene -- he's on the phone, listening
to some very shitty news. THREE OTHER ATTORNEYS perched
phones around the room. Some major crisis --

> BARRY
> ...Jesus...Jesus...<u>Jesus</u>...
> (listening)
> ...this was...oh, <u>Jesus</u>...Jesus...
> (each pause more painful)
> ...Jesus...<u>oh, Jesus</u>...
> (looking up and--)
> ...hang on --
> (a savior)
> -- there you are!

MICHAEL in the doorway. All eyes rushing to him --

> MICHAEL
> What's up?

> BARRY
> <u>Arthur Edens just stripped down naked
> in a deposition room in Milwaukee.</u>

EXT. TETERBORO AIRPORT -- DAY

Fifty one minutes later. MICHAEL crossing the tarmac toward
a private jet, as we begin to hear the familiar express train
chatter of --

> ARTHUR EDENS (V.O.)
> ...even this, Michael -- even now --
> that you're here -- there's a reason,
> a reason it's you -- <u>every</u> reason --
> surely you can sense that -- how it
> pulls together -- how it gathers --
> Nurse Michael -- Secret Hero -- Keeper
> of the Hidden Sins -- tell me you can
> see that, Michael, for God's sake...
> (continuing, as--)

EXT. MILWAUKEE ATRIUM HOTEL -- DAY

The big one out near the airport. And it's SNOWING. <u>Hard</u>.
Starting to really come down --

> ARTHUR EDENS (V.O.)
> ...and <u>yes</u> -- I mean, okay, the nudity
> -- the parking lot -- I admit it --
> <u>mistake</u>! It was wrong. It was lame.
> It was obvious. And frankly, for me,
> (MORE)

                    ARTHUR EDENS (V.O.) (cont'd)
          therapeutically, it was useless,
          because Michael, I swear, if I stood
          there and peeled off my fucking <u>skin</u>
          I couldn't get down to where this
          thing is living...

A LUXURY VAN whipping up to the entrance. KAREN and her two
assistants, MAUDE and TODD, exiting the vehicle. This a
well-practiced, military drill: MAUDE rushing for an assault
on the front desk. TODD flanking with the luggage and gear.

                    ARTHUR EDENS (V.O.)
          ...Six years, Michael! Six years
          I've absorbed this poison! Six years --
          four hundred depositions -- a hundred
          motions -- five changes of venue --
          eighty-four thousand documents in
          discovery!

KAREN wasting not a moment, working a cell phone and a call
sheet -- a tightened jaw her only surrender to the urgency
and crisis of the moment --

                    ARTHUR EDENS (V.O.)
          ...Six years I've steered this beast,
          Michael -- six years of stalling and
          screaming and scheming and...

<u>INT. MILWAUKEE JAIL HOLDING CELL -- NIGHT</u>

A shabby, ugly pisshole. Two chairs. No air. <u>ARTHUR EDENS</u>
in the flesh. Late fifties. Brilliance and grace amidst the
manic shambles.

                    ARTHUR
          Look at me, Michael. Twelve percent
          of my life has been spent protecting
          the reputation of a deadly weedkiller!

                    MICHAEL
               (sitting there)
          We had an agreement, Arthur.

                    ARTHUR
               (oblivious)
          -- one night, right? -- I look up
          and Marty's standing in my office
          with a bottle of champagne --

                    MICHAEL
          <u>Do you remember our agreement?</u>

                    ARTHUR
          -- I know, just let me -- <u>just</u> --
               (he simply can't stop)
          -- he tells me we've just hit thirty-
          thousand billable hours on U/North
          and he wants to celebrate. An hour
          later, I'm in a whorehouse in Chelsea
          and two Lithuanian redheads are taking
          turns sucking my dick. I'm laying
          there, I'm trying not to come, I'm
          trying to make it last, right? So I
          start doing the math -- thirty thousand
          hours -- what is that? -- twenty-four
          times thirty -- seven-hundred twenty
          hours in a month -- eight-thousand-
          seven-hundred and sixty hours per
          year...

                    MICHAEL
          <u>Arthur</u>.

                    ARTHUR
          <u>Wait</u>!
               (on his feet now, pacing,
                faster and faster--)
          Because it's years -- it's <u>lives</u> --
          and the numbers are making me dizzy,
          and now, now I'm not just trying not
          to come, I'm trying not to <u>think</u>!
          But I can't stop! Is that me? Am I
          just some freak organism that's been
          put here to eat and sleep and spend
          my days defending this one horrific
          chain of carcinogenic molecules?
          Is that my destiny? Is this is my
          place?

                    MICHAEL
          You promised me, Arthur.

                    ARTHUR
          <u>Is that it, Michael</u>?
               (edgy suddenly)
          Is that my grail? Two Lithuanian
          mouths on my cock? Is that the correct
          answer to the multiple choice of me?

     MICHAEL grabs him -- <u>hard</u> -- pulling him close --

                    MICHAEL
          You want to go off your medication?
          Fine. But you call me first.
               (face-to-face)
          <u>That was our agreement</u>.

ARTHUR staring back. Eyes wild. Euphoric.

                    ARTHUR
          Sue me.

CRACK! -- MICHAEL startled -- behind him -- A MILWAUKEE JAIL
GUARD rapping on the bars --

                    JAIL GUARD
          We okay in there?

                    MICHAEL
               (letting Arthur go)
          We're fine.

THE JAIL GUARD hesitates. Moves on.

                    ARTHUR
               (whispering now)
          They killed these people, Michael.
          Little farms. Family farms. This
          girl, Anna, did you see her?

                    MICHAEL
          No.

                    ARTHUR
          You need to see her. Talk to her.
          She's a miracle. She's is God's
          perfect creature. And for fifty
          million dollars in fees I have spent
          twelve percent of my life destroying
          perfect Anna and her dead parents
          and her dying brother.

MICHAEL pulls a prescription bottle from his pocket --

                    MICHAEL
          When's the last time you took one of
          these?

                    ARTHUR
          No. I'm not losing this.
               (backing away)
          Everything is finally significant.
          The world is radiant and beautiful and
          you want me to trade that for this?

                    MICHAEL
          If it's real, the pill won't kill it.

                    ARTHUR
          I have blood on my hands.

                         MICHAEL
          You are a Senior Litigating Partner
          at one of the largest, most respected
          law firms in the world. You are a
          legend.

                         ARTHUR
          I'm an accomplice.

                         MICHAEL
          You're a manic depressive.

                         ARTHUR
          I'm Shiva the God of death.

                         MICHAEL
          Let's get out of Milwaukee and we'll
          talk about it.

INT. MILWAUKEE HOTEL CONFERENCE ROOM -- DAY

VIDEO FOOTAGE. Deposition in progress. Drab room. Drab
vibe. HALF-A-DOZEN ATTORNEYS on either side of a table.
Perhaps we glimpse a face or two, but the camera's angle is
set to feature the witness -- ANNA KYSURSEN is twenty-three
years old. Big. And blonde. Cream skinned. Ripe. Open.
Plain. Arthur's dairy madonna.

                         ANNA
          ...we came back from the hospital and
          everybody was crying and we were in
          shock, but we still, we had to milk.

                         LAWYER'S VOICE
          The cows won't wait will they?

                         ANNA
          No.

                         LAWYER'S VOICE
          And when you went to the barn...

                         ANNA
          We found the note. My sister found it.

                         LAWYER'S VOICE
          From your mother.

                         ANNA
          Yes.

                         LAWYER'S VOICE
          Could you read it for us?

ANNA fighting back an onslaught of emotion, finds a piece of
paper there in front of her.

                    LAWYER'S VOICE
        Anna?
            (Anna looks up, hands
            shaking--)
        Why don't you just read us the third
        paragraph -- just the highlighted
        section there.

ANNA nods. Bearing down. But it's tough...

                       ANNA
        "I don't want you blaming Ned Hardy, or
        any of the people down at the feedlot.
        They're just farmers themselves.
        U/North fooled them just as bad as us
        and Ned has had enough pain already..."
            (but now she's crying--)

                    LAWYER'S VOICE
        Anna?

Suddenly, another voice explodes through the room --

                    ARTHUR
        ANNA, I'M SORRY! I LOVE YOU! I'M
        SORRY! I'M SO VERY VERY SORRY!

For a moment there's this weird paralyzed silence -- everyone
too stunned to react -- everyone except for ARTHUR -- he's
standing and we're sort of seeing him from the back -- seeing
him rip his shirt away from his body and --

                ANOTHER LAWYER'S VOICE
        -- what the hell is he? -- what're you
        doing? --

                    AND ANOTHER
        -- omigod, he's --

                    AND ANOTHER
        -- Arthur? -- ARTHUR! --

                    ARTHUR
        I LOVE YOU, ANNA! AND I'M SORRY!
        I'M SO VERY VERY SORRY! I LOVE YOU!

Instant chaos -- <u>motion</u> -- VOICES YELLING -- THE CAMERA
JOSTLED -- someone's throwing a punch -- ARTHUR still
stripping and struggling and begging for forgiveness, and
then, suddenly, it all goes black as we REVERSE TO --

INT.   KAREN'S MILWAUKEE HOTEL SUITE -- NIGHT

KAREN staring at a blank VIDEO MONITOR.

                    TODD
               (with the remote)
          I guess that's it.

KAREN stands. Ashen. Silent. Outside, through the window
we can see the snow pouring down --

                    KAREN
          They close O'Hare?

MAUDE across the room. Sitting at a quickly assembled
communications desk. Laptops, printers, wireless antennae --

                    MAUDE
          Four minutes ago. There's a foot
          of snow in Detroit already...

                    KAREN
          You have Don?

                    MAUDE
          Still with the board.

                    KAREN
          Who's the guy they sent from New York?
          Clayton. I never heard of him.

INT. MILWAUKEE POLICE PRECINCT HOLDING DESK -- NIGHT

Active. MILWAUKEE COPS coming and going. Snow on boots.
Snow out the window. MICHAEL in his wheelhouse, chatting up
a DESK SERGEANT AND LIEUTENANT as --

                    MAUDE (V.O.)
          Michael Raymond Clayton. Born
          September nine, 1959, St. Joseph's
          Hospital, Bronx, New York...

INT. MILWAUKEE HOLDING CELL OUTER AREA -- NIGHT

TWO GUARDS processing ARTHUR out of his cell.

                    MAUDE (V.O.)
          ...Father is NYPD Patrolman, Raymond
          Xavier Clayton, twenty-six. Mother,
          Alice Mary Clayton, twenty-three...

INT. MILWAUKEE POLICE PRECINCT DESK AREA -- NIGHT

MICHAEL with a cellphone. Someone important on the line.
Handing the phone over to A POLICE CAPTAIN as --

                    MAUDE (V.O.)
        ...Graduates Washingtonville Central
        High School, Orange County New York in
        1977. Graduates St. John's University,
        1980. Fordham Law, '82....

INT. MILWAUKEE HOLDING CELL OUTER AREA -- NIGHT

ARTHUR smiling -- beaming -- as THE GUARDS process him out.

                    MAUDE (V.O.)
        ...'82 through '86 he's an ADA with
        the Queens District Attorney's
        Office...

INT. MILWAUKEE POLICE PRECINCT DESK AREA -- NIGHT

MICHAEL all smiles as A YOUNG PROSECUTOR arrives. She's got
Arthur's paperwork, MICHAEL turning on the charm, getting her
to smile as --

                    MAUDE (V.O.)
        ...1986 he's with a Joint Manhattan-
        Queens Organized Crime Task Force.
        And then, 1990 he starts at Kenner,
        Bach & Ledeen.

INT. KAREN'S MILWAUKEE HOTEL SUITE -- NIGHT

MAUDE at her screens. KAREN over her shoulder --

                    KAREN
        So he's a partner.

                    MAUDE
        Nope. He's listed as "Special
        Counsel." Says he specializes in
        Wills and Trusts.

                    KAREN
        He goes from criminal prosecution to
        Wills and Trusts? He's there thirteen
        years he's not a partner? And he's
        the guy they sent?
            (reading it again)
        Who is this guy?

INT/EXT. MILWAUKEE POLICE PRECINCT -- NIGHT

MICHAEL, TWO MILWAUKEE POLICEMEN and ELSTON leading a smiling
ARTHUR out of the building -- toward/into the snow and a
waiting MILWAUKEE POLICE CRUISER.

INT. ASSOCIATES MILWAUKEE HOTEL SUITE -- NIGHT

Temporary Milwaukee home of Kenner Bach & Ledeen. More dorm
room than office. Pizza boxes. Masses of paper. Boomboxes
and laptops. Gym clothes and garment bags and --

                    MICHAEL
          So none of you, nobody had any idea
          he was coming.
               (he's talking to--)

FOUR YOUNG LAWYERS. Two first year associates. One third
year. One fifth. Familiar faces from the deposition video.

                    THIRD YEAR
               (are you kidding?)
          To Milwaukee? For a deposition?

                    FIFTH YEAR
          We thought maybe there was some kind
          of settlement in the works. There's
          been some rumors, so we thought maybe
          he was here for that, but...

                    MICHAEL
          Who talked to him?

                    FIRST YEAR
          I did.
               (nervous)
          He just said he wanted to depose
          this girl Anna. And could he borrow
          some headphones.

                    MICHAEL
          All right, look...
               (he's heard enough)
          This is very simple. Arthur's got a
          chemical imbalance. He's supposed to
          be on medication. He fell behind
          with that. He's back on the mend.
          He'll be fine in three, four days.

MICHAEL letting that sink in a moment. Now the hammer.

                    MICHAEL
          What happened here stays in this
          room. This is not a piece of
                    (MORE)

                    MICHAEL (cont'd)
information you want to be out in
front of. Anybody has a problem with
that let me know right now.
          (dead silence)
We're stuck here overnight. I'm gonna
get him home tomorrow if I can. Who's
in charge of the deposition schedule?

                    THIRD YEAR
I am.

                    MICHAEL
Where does it stand?

                    THIRD YEAR
I guess it's on hold. We didn't know
exactly what to--

                    MICHAEL
Nothing's on hold. You just do what
you were planning on doing. The other
side wants to talk about it, let them
call New York, okay?
          (four heads bobbing--)
And I need his briefcase.

                    FIFTH YEAR
Arthur's? I don't...

                    MICHAEL
He says he left it in the room.

                    FIRST YEAR
It might be with the stuff Jody
grabbed...

The search through the clutter has begun and --

                    MICHAEL
Find it.

INT. HENRY CLAYTON'S BEDROOM -- NIGHT

THE CAMERA moving over a collage of fantasy images: Posters,
postcards; magazine pages and book covers; fantasy landscapes
and fantasy castles, fantasy characters, journeys and
battles, as we hear...

                    HENRY (OS)
...so all these people, they all start
having these dreams, okay? You know
what a vision quest is? Like for
Navahos and stuff?

> ARTHUR (PHONE/OVER)
> (thick with thorazine)
> I think so. Like a special dream.

> HENRY (OS)
> Except this is like a whole bunch of
> people having the _same_ dream. They're
> all having this dream that they should
> go to this one place. They don't know
> why or anything, they just have this
> feeling that they have to go there.

> ARTHUR (PHONE/OVER)
> That they've been summoned.

HENRY IN HIS LOFT BED. On the phone. Past his bedtime.

> HENRY
> That's the chapter! That's what
> it's called. "Summons to Conquest."
> Seriously, that's the title.

INT. MICHAEL'S MILWAUKEE HOTEL BEDROOM -- NIGHT (CONT)

ARTHUR EDENS alone in a dark hotel room bed. Doped up.

> ARTHUR
> Do they know? Do they know they're
> all having the same dream?

> HENRY (PHONE/OVER)
> No, that's what's so cool, they all
> think it's just them, that maybe
> they're like going crazy or something
> so they don't want to admit it.

> ARTHUR
> But they're not crazy, are they?

INT. HENRY CLAYTON'S BEDROOM -- NIGHT

> HENRY
> No, it's real. It's really happening.

> ARTHUR (PHONE/OVER)
> It _is_ happening, isn't it? Something
> larger than themselves, they're just
> not ready, are they, to hear it --"

> HENRY
> -- yeah, but then later they do, so
> if you're gonna read it, I don't want
> to spoil it --
> (stopping because--)

GERALD (stepfather) standing at the bedroom doorway.

                    GERALD
          -- what are you doing? -- who're
          you talking to?

                    HENRY
          -- I called my dad's room -- some
          friend of dad's --

                    GERALD
          -- it's like ten-thirty, Henry --

INT. MICHAEL'S MILWAUKEE HOTEL BEDROOM -- NIGHT

                    ARTHUR
               (frantic suddenly)
          -- Hello... Hello? --
               (he can hear them arguing
                in the BG--)

                    HENRY (PHONE/OVER)
          I gotta get off now.

                    ARTHUR
          -- wait! -- the book -- I need the
          book -- the title -- and you, I don't
          know your name...

                    HENRY (PHONE/OVER)
          I'm Henry. The book is called Realm
          and Conquest.

                    ARTHUR
               (fumbling for a pen)
          Realm and Conquest.

                    HENRY (PHONE/OVER)
          It's Book One with a red cover.
               (Gerald pressing in
                the background--)
          I gotta go -- tell my dad I called,
          okay?

                    ARTHUR
          Thank you, Henry. Thank you.
             (dial tone)
          Thank you.
             (silence)
          Thank you.

INT. MILWAUKEE HOTEL LOBBY/BAR -- NIGHT

MICHAEL enters. It's late. He's late. BARTENDER starting
to cash out. MICHAEL sees KAREN working across the room.

INT. MILWAUKEE BAR/TABLE -- NIGHT

KARTEN looks up as MICHAEL arrives. He's got two drinks.

                    MICHAEL
          There you are. Sorry I'm late.

                    KAREN
          Where is he?

                    MICHAEL
          He's asleep. He's out cold.
               (offering the drink)
          He's closing up the register...

                    KAREN
               (not having it)
          Tell me this was some kind of strategy.

                    MICHAEL
          Wouldn't that be nice.

                    KAREN
          You saw this tape? The video?

                    MICHAEL
          I heard about it.

                    KAREN
          What happened after was worse.

                    MICHAEL
          He'll be fine once he's back on the
          medication.

But she's not listening. She's flipping through a notepad --

                    KAREN
          This was in the parking lot, okay?
          These people are running for their
          cars, he's got nothing on but his
          socks, and whatever the hell your team
          was doing to stop this was clearly not
          working, because --
               (reading her notes)
          "I'm sorry. I'm so sorry. I will not
          sit with this sickness any longer.
          I cannot aid this sickness any longer."
                    (MORE)

                         KAREN   (cont'd)
                    (incredulous)
          What does that mean?

                         MICHAEL
          I'm not really sure.

                         KAREN
          You've been with him all evening.
          What's he been saying?

                         MICHAEL
          Not much.
                    (flat out lying)
          We got him sedated pretty quickly.

                         KAREN
          This is totally unacceptable, you
          realize that the --

                         MICHAEL
          -- once he's back on the medication,
          it's really just a matter of--

                         KAREN
          -- this is a three-billion dollar
          class-action lawsuit! Tomorrow morning
          I have to call my board and tell them
          the architect of our entire defense was
          arrested running naked in a snowstorm
          chasing the plaintiffs through a
          parking lot!

                         MICHAEL
          I understand.

                         KAREN
          What "sickness" is he talking about?

                         MICHAEL
          Could be a lot of things.

                         KAREN
          Name one.

                         MICHAEL
          Frostbite?

                         KAREN
          You think this is funny?

                         MICHAEL
          Look, his wife was sick, she died
          last year. His daughter doesn't talk
          to him. He's all alone. All he does
                         (MORE)

                        MICHAEL (cont'd)
          is your case. He skipped his pills.
          He had a bad day. It's that simple.

                        KAREN
          And you're an authority on this?

                        MICHAEL
          His last episode was eight years ago.
          I was there. I helped bring him home.
          I watched him get better.
               (beat)
          I mean, c'mon...you didn't hire Arthur
          for his low-key regularity. You took
          him because he's a killer and he's
          brilliant and he's just crazy enough
          to grind away on a case like this for
          six years without a break.

                        KAREN
          Excuse me, but we pay for his time.

                        MICHAEL
          I thought you wanted an explanation.

KAREN folds the notebook. Steely silence.

                        KAREN
          I'm calling Marty Bach in the morning.
          But then you know that...

MICHAEL nods. Understood.

INT. MICHAEL'S MILWAUKEE HOTEL SITTING ROOM -- NIGHT

THE POLICE LT. (ELSTON) -- the guy Michael was glad-handing
in the precinct -- pulling on his parka getting ready to go
home.

                        ELSTON
          He was mostly just quiet. I heard
          him moving around, I gave him the
          other pill about fifteen minutes ago.

MICHAEL taking off his jacket. Pulling a nice, thick
envelope from the pocket. Time to pay the babysitter --

                        MICHAEL
          I really appreciate it, Elston.
               (handing it over--)
          You get to New York, you know you're
          coming -- you need tickets, a game,
          whatever, give me a heads up.

                    ELSTON
        I'll do that for sure.

INT. MICHAEL'S MILWAUKEE HOTEL BEDROOM -- NIGHT

A minute later. MICHAEL enters. It's quiet. Dark. Dim
light from the bathroom. MICHAEL pulls off his tie. What
a fucking day. Taking off his watch, when --

                    ARTHUR
                (voice from the bed)
        Did you see her?

                    MICHAEL
        Who?

                    ARTHUR
        Anna.

ARTHUR bleary and soporific. Beached there.

                    MICHAEL
        Anna? No. No, I didn't see her.
            (like you'd talk to
            a child)
        She probably went back to the farm.

                    ARTHUR
        We need her.

MICHAEL nods. Barely listening. Kicking off his shoes.

                    ARTHUR
        Marty. Even then. The rest of them.
        They won't understand.

                    MICHAEL
            (just humoring him)
        Don't worry, Arthur, if anybody can
        explain it to them, it's you.

                    ARTHUR
        No. They're lost. They have what
        they want.

                    MICHAEL
        Let it go, man. Get some sleep.

Silence now. MICHAEL moves to the window. Standing there.
Pulling the curtain. Loosening his collar. Watching snow
fall across the parking lot. When, suddenly --

                    ARTHUR
                (loud and clear)
            Is this what you wanted?

ARTHUR there in the half-light. Sitting up. Defying the
medication. Sheer will.

                    ARTHUR
            Be a janitor? Live like this?
            Do this? What you do...

MICHAEL caught off-guard. Not prepared for clarity.

                    ARTHUR
            It can't be. That I know this.
            The burden. That's what I'm telling
            you.
                (weakening)
            How it feels. That I know...
                (going fast)
            That we've been summoned...

MICHAEL not sure what to say, or if there's even anybody
listening, because ARTHUR is already sloping back into the
pillows; already drifting back under the medication's
gravitational pull and...

MICHAEL alone now. Standing there at the window. Shaken.

INT. KAREN'S MILWAUKEE HOTEL SUITE -- NIGHT

ARTHUR EDEN'S BRIEFCASE. Bathed in the light of a hotel
desk lamp. The initials A.D.E. embossed in the worn, old
leather. THE CAMERA MOVING across the desk, as we hear the
sound of a PHONE RINGING THROUGH THE LINE and --

                    VERNE (PHONE/OVER)
            Hello?

                    KAREN (OS)
                (tense, tentative)
            Yes. Hi. I'm looking for Vern?

THE CONTENTS OF THE BRIEFCASE arranged in piles around the
desk. A chaotic mix of legal documents, bizarre books, and
a few odd, found objects --

                    VERNE (PHONE/OVER)
            You have a number?

                    KAREN (OS)
            Don Jeffries gave it to me, he said
            I could call anytime...

47

                    VERNE (PHONE/OVER)
         The account number.

                    KAREN (OS)
         The code. Yes. Sorry. I have it...
              (papers rustling in the
              background, as--)

THE CAMERA FEATURES -- A TWENTY-PAGE DOCUMENT -- at the
center of everything. Space on the desk cleared around it.
It's a photocopy, dated, June, 19, 1991. On the cover...

UNITED-NORTHFIELD
CULCITATE -- INTERNAL RESEARCH MEMORANDUM #229

And there's no need to get into the text of this memo right
now. It is, however, important that we feel the *extreme*
danger and power this document has for KAREN.

                    KAREN (OS)
         ...okay, it's twelve-B-K-R-6.

KAREN holding the phone with one hand, the other covered with
an improvised glove made from a plastic hotel laundry bag --

                    KAREN
         Am I speaking with Vern?

                    VERNE (PHONE/OVER)
         Mister Verne.

                    KAREN
         I'm sorry it's so late. Don said
         just...I'm not really...I don't know
         how this works so...

                    VERNE (PHONE/OVER)
         You have e-mail at your current
         location?

                    KAREN
         Yes.

                    VERNE (PHONE/OVER)
         I'm gonna upload you a little
         encryption package we like. It's
         pretty self-explanatory.

                    KAREN
         Okay.

                    VERNE (PHONE/OVER)
         Let me get to my desk.

She's on hold. The "gloved" hand reaches down for the memo
there at the center of it all. Her eyes scan the words, as
if maybe his time they'll be different. They're not.
She catches her reflection now in the mirror over the desk.
Frozen like that. Waiting, as --

INT. MICHAEL'S MILWAUKEE HOTEL SITTING ROOM -- DAY

Morning. The storm is over. MICHAEL has showered. He's
drinking room service coffee, pacing around on a cell phone --

                    MICHAEL
          ...no, I know. We were...we just
          couldn't stay open.
               (impatient pause)
          Yeah, what I'm wondering, I've got
          an option on the lease for six more
          years. You know the space, I'm
          wondering if you think there's any
          chance I could lay that off? Is the
          lease worth anything?
               (pause)
          Eighty-nine hundred a month. I
          mean, the fixtures are gone, but
          the bar, the kitchen, it's great
          space...

MICHAEL listening and it's not the answer he was hoping for.
And he's pacing around, taking us toward the bedroom doors.
One open, the other one closed. THE SOUND OF THE SHOWER
running from the other room --

                    MICHAEL
               (finally)
          No...no, I hear you. I just...
               (pause)
          Yup. You got it. Thanks anyway.
               (beat)
          I will.

MICHAEL hangs up. Numb. Trying to shake it off.

                    MICHAEL
               (checking his watch)
          Let's go, Arthur!

No answer. MICHAEL starts to turn away. Then he stops.

                    MICHAEL
          Arthur!
               (he tries the door, it's
               locked--)
          Arthur! You hear me? Open the door.
               (MORE)

                              MICHAEL (cont'd)
                        (banging on it now--)
                    Open the goddam door, Arthur!
                        (harder)
                    ARTHUR!   OPEN THE DOOR!

Because suddenly, the anger has transformed into fear --
he's trying the door again -- <u>really</u> trying it --

                              MICHAEL
                    ARTHUR, CAN YOU HEAR ME?

MICHAEL rearing back -- coming in hard now and --

                              MICHAEL
                    -- shit! --
                        (he just banged the hell
                        out of his shoulder--)
                    GODDAMIT, ARTHUR!

The body slam was useless, but it's not an impossible door
-- he's standing back -- clutching his shoulder -- kicking
as hard as he can near the knob and --

THE DOOR groans -- gives a little -- MICHAEL kicking again --
now it SPLINTERS -- MICHAEL giving it everything this time
and this time THE DOOR shatters off its hinges, still sort of
hanging there as MICHAEL pushes and claws it away, rushing
now into --

INT. MICHAEL'S MILWAUKEE HOTEL SUITE/BATHROOM -- DAY

MICHAEL stopping cold. The shower is running and nobody's in
there. Written on the mirror in shaving cream:

MAKE BELIEVE IT'S NOT JUST MADNESS!

MICHAEL backing out -- rushing into --

INT. MICHAEL'S MILWAUKEE HOTEL BEDROOM

Window open. Curtain wafting in the wind. ARTHUR is gone.

EXT. MIAMI GOLF CLUB -- DAY

A CORPORATE LOGO -- embossed on a high-quality, golf bag:

u/north
"we grow your world together"

WIDER TO REVEAL

THE PRO-SHOP/BAG DROP of a first-class golf club. It's a
gorgeous, sunny morning. A CADDY reaching in -- shouldering
the bag --

                         CADDY
               Not playing today, Mr. Verne?

MR. VERNE turns. He's one of those guys who looks like he's
been in his late forties forever. Trim but solid. Tan and
clean. Pressed and fresh. Every piece of gear in place.

                         VERNE
               Yeah, we had a change in plan...
                    (pointing out to the
                     parking lot--)
               That's gonna go in the Navigator.
               The black one. It's open.

THE CADDY starts for the car, as MR. IKER comes out of the
locker room. IKER is a slightly younger version of Mr.
Verne. Country club slacks. Good loafers. Hands and
forearms that speak of deeper experience than the back nine.

                         IKER
               You want anything for the road?
               They've got that great fruit salad...

                         VERNE
                    (checking his watch)
               Naw, we better hit it.

INT.   LAW FIRM/MARTY BACH'S OFFICE -- DAY

MARTY BACH at his desk. In his hands, a copy of U/NORTH
RESEARCH MEMO #229. ARTHUR'S BRIEFCASE open beside him.

KAREN watching him read. Just the two of them. And the
silence is deafening. Finally, he finishes. Like a doctor
holding a malignant X-ray...

                         MARTY
               That's really Don's signature?
                    (she nods)
               Where's the original?

                         KAREN
               We had an unfortunate warehouse fire
               five years ago. We lost a number of
               documents.

MARTY hesitates. *Okay*...

                    MARTY
          How does this end up in Arthur's bag?

                    KAREN
          There's a three billion dollar
          question for you.

INT.   LAW FIRM/ARTHUR EDEN'S OFFICE -- NIGHT

A SILVER FRAMED PHOTOGRAPH. Young Arthur Edens with his
wife and baby daughter. Some faded happy moment. This one
of several very traditional items, on a very traditional
desk. In fact the whole place is almost disturbingly
repressed. The only thing out of place are the dozens of
document boxes piled at the center of the room.

MARTY and BARRY GRISSOM digging through all of it. Like
they've been at it a while.

                    MARTY
          I want all this -- everything here
          -- I want it all boxed up and sent
          to my apartment.

MICHAEL in the doorway. Watching them plunder. Until --

                    MARTY
               (without looking back)
          Any luck, Michael?

BARRY turns, surprised. MICHAEL steps into the office.

                    MICHAEL
          He booked a limo from Newark airport
          at three. He got out at West Fourth
          Street, tipped the driver fifty bucks,
          and walked away.

                    MARTY
          You try his place?

                    MICHAEL
          It's a loft. There's no doorman.
          I rang, nobody answered. I call,
          I get the machine.

                    BARRY
               (thanks for nothing)
          So basically, he could be anywhere...

MICHAEL bites his tongue. No love lost with Barry.

                    MARTY
Arthur downtown was not a good idea.
Some goddam loft?

                    BARRY
Where's his daughter?

                    MICHAEL
He's not sure. Spain? India?

                    MARTY
Mars.
        (putting down the
        photograph--)
She's crazier than he'll ever be.
        (to Michael)
Barry's going to take over on U/North.
We've all got a lot of grovelling to
do with these people.
        (pointedly)
You didn't exactly charm Karen Crowder.

                    MICHAEL
I was punting.

                    BARRY
You've got to saddle up here, Michael,
and get this under control.

                    MICHAEL
Saddle up?

                    BARRY
He needs to be under a doctor's care
immediately. He needs to be admitted.

                    MICHAEL
Where?

                    BARRY
Does it matter?

                    MARTY
Michael...
        (the voice of reason)
U/North needs to know that he's under
control. That he's in a facility.
They've been shaken up, they need to
be reassured.

                    MICHAEL
It's just not gonna be that easy.

                         BARRY
          Why the hell not?

                         MICHAEL
          Because the laws in the State Of New
          York set a pretty high threshold for
          involuntary commitment.

                         BARRY
          Did you see this fucking tape?

                         MICHAEL
          I'm not arguing with you, Barry, I'm
          telling you how it is.

                         MARTY
          You know what? We've got six hundred
          attorneys in this building. Let's find
          out which one of them knows the most
          about psychiatric commitment statutes.

                         MICHAEL
          I can tell you that right now.
               (beat)
          It's Arthur.

Smiling. As we hear --

                         IKER (RADIO/OVER)
          "Okay. I'm in. We're good to go."

EXT. NEW YORK STREET #1 -- NIGHT

ARTHUR walking. Bathing in the miracle of it all. His eyes
seem locked open, gathering stimuli faster than the speed of
light. Every moment -- every beatific instant -- has a
purpose. Everything is fuel for the significance turbine
spinning inside him. Passing into the night, as --

THE CAMERA FINDS -- VERNE fifty yards behind ARTHUR. Tailing
him. Looking like just another nightcrawler doing the cell
phone walk-and-talk --

                         VERNE
               (into his microphone)
          "Roger that. Let's keep a radio
          check every five, okay?"

INT. ELEVATOR LANDING/ARTHUR'S LOFT -- NIGHT (CONT)

A downtown building. IKER standing at the door to Arthur's
loft. Backpack. Tool kit. Same radio/cellphone rig.
Gloved hands, already starting to work the lock, as --

                              IKER
                      (into his microphone)
                   "Every five. Roger that."

INT. MICHAEL'S APARTMENT/BEDROOM -- NIGHT

Clean, slick bachelor decor. MICHAEL with a towel wrapped at
his waist, sits at the edge of the bed, speed dialing a
mobile phone. The sheets with an apres-sex chaos about them.

                         ARTHUR'S VOICE
                     (his answering machine)
                   "You've reached Arthur. If you wish to
                   leave a message, please do so after the
                   tone."

MICHAEL hangs up before the beep.

                            BRINI (OS)
                      (from the kitchen)
                   You want me to heat it up?

                             MICHAEL
                      (calling back)
                   Doesn't matter.

INT. MICHAEL'S APARTMENT/KITCHEN -- NIGHT (CONT)

BRINI GLASS -- the young lawyer we met in the elevator at
Kenner, Bach -- is busy reheating a Chinese takeout dinner
that was obviously interrupted earlier. She's wearing
nothing but one of Michael's shirts.

It's a modern, one-bedroom apartment in a high-rise that
towers over Columbus Avenue. The kitchen open to the living
room. Windows to Central Park and The Westside twenty
stories below. A slick pad. Small but clean, furnished
efficiently, and the view is sharp.

BRINI starts the microwave. There's a roach in an ashtray
on the counter. She lights it. Taking a drag, as MICHAEL
wanders in from the bedroom.

                             BRINI
                      (the joint)
                   You want?

He waves it off. Coming around behind her. Kissing her
neck as he moves to the refrigerator.

                             MICHAEL
                   Now you're hungry...

                    BRINI
          I know.

There's an open bottle of white wine. He's pouring.

                    MICHAEL
          You never told me you were working
          with Jeff Gaffney.

                    BRINI
          It's just a project.
               (pulling plates from
               the cupboard--)
          He hates you. You know that, right?

                    MICHAEL
          There's a heartbreaker.

                    BRINI
          You helped him out, didn't you?

                    MICHAEL
          Jeff Gaffney hates everyone.

                    BRINI
          What did you do for him?

                    MICHAEL
          I don't even remember.

                    BRINI
          That is such bullshit...

He just smiles. She tries the wine. Some subtle tension
pulling at her. And the dope didn't get her where she
wanted.

                    BRINI
          I watch these people. At the office.
          How they relate to you. I can always
          tell, or I think I can anyway, the ones
          that you've done something for.

                    MICHAEL
          Half of them don't even know I work
          there.

                    BRINI
          Or they're pretending to ignore you,
          or else they're super polite...

                    MICHAEL
          Or they hate me.

He looks at her. She looks away.

> BRINI
>
> I never know what you know or don't
> know.

> MICHAEL
>
> Try me.

> BRINI
>
> They offered me London.
>   (awkward beat)
> Or did you know that already?

> MICHAEL
>
> No. I didn't know that.

> BRINI
>
> I wasn't sure.

> MICHAEL
>
> So this is the merger.

> BRINI
>
> I can't believe you don't know all
> this.
>   (trying to laugh it off--)
> Well, there you go... I'm blown.
> There's my big secret.

> MICHAEL
>
> I thought I was your secret.

> BRINI
>
> Really? I always thought it was the
> other way around.

The microwave starts beeping.

> MICHAEL
>
> I was gonna say when were you gonna
> tell me, but I guess that's what you're
> doing.

> BRINI
>
> I really thought you knew.

MICHAEL looks away. Something catching his eye.

THERE ON THE COUNTER

"REALM AND CONQUEST." Book One. The red cover. MICHAEL
picking it up. A momentary distraction.

> BRINI
> I haven't decided yet either.
>   (trying a smile)
> Seriously. Nothing's been decided.

She's waiting for him to answer. He hesitates. Puts the
book down.

> MICHAEL
> Jeff Gaffney's wife starts this affair
> with their contractor in East Hampton.
> It takes about a month, the guy
> realizes she's crazy, he tries to break
> it off. She gets drunk. She drives
> out to his house, takes a road flare
> and tries to torch his truck. She's
> just so fucked up she doesn't see the
> two Dominican kids sleeping in the
> garage. One guy it turned out okay.
> The other one needed a lot of help.

Was that a gift or a bomb? Neither of them sure.

> BRINI
> Jesus...
>   (staring at him)
> How do you make something like that
> disappear?
>   (off his silence)
> I guess you don't.

MICHAEL drains his wine. Pouring another, as --

EXT. NEW YORK STREET #2 -- NIGHT

ARTHUR marching through the night. Same glorious smile.
Just another madman loose in Manhattan.

INT. ARTHUR'S LOFT -- NIGHT

A DIGITAL CAMERA LCD SCREEN. THE IMAGE -- an overhead shot
of a coffee table cluttered with magazines, newspapers and
junk mail.

THE DIGITAL CAMERA is sitting on THE ACTUAL COFFEE TABLE.
IKER, wearing gloves and a hair net, is very precisely and
quickly searching through the debris. A consummate
professional at work. As he proceeds, he keeps checking the
camera image to make sure every object is returned to its
original position.

This is raw space. A box. High ceilings. Industrial
windows along one wall. Half-assed groupings of furniture
define the space: Bed and dresser, desk and computer,

bathroom and closets framed out along the far walls.
The decor is odd. Half the stuff is clearly from a previous
life; Eastside antiques, proper rugs, generic oil landscapes
piled carelessly around. Above all this, the clutter of
Arthur's recent manic acquisitions -- books, papers, found
objects, curios -- as if a layer of madness were blanketing
the landscape of his old life.

IKER MOVING THROUGH THE LOFT -- eyes scanning -- barely
reacting as -- <u>THE PHONE RINGS</u> -- and he begins to hear:

> ARTHUR'S VOICE
> (on the answering machine)
> "If you wish to leave a message, please
> do so after the tone."
> (<u>beep</u>, and then--)

> MICHAEL'S VOICE
> (through the machine)
> Arthur, look, I've been calling all
> day, if you're there, please for
> crissake just pick up and talk to me...
> (continuing as--)

INT. MICHAEL'S APARTMENT/BEDROOM -- NIGHT

BRINI alone in bed. Deep asleep.

> MICHAEL (PHONE/OVER)
> No? Yes? Shit, come on, man...
> (a weary beat)
> Arthur, listen to me, I'm leaving my
> phone on -- we <u>have</u> to talk...
> (continuing, as--)

INT. MICHAEL'S APARTMENT/LIVING ROOM -- NIGHT

MICHAEL in the dark with the phone and a new bottle of wine.

> MICHAEL
> ...what happened this morning --
> yesterday morning -- whatever it is --
> forget it, okay? Someday we'll laugh
> about it, right? But you gotta get
> back to me here, okay? And soon.
> (about to hang up, when--)
> Arthur, look...I'll tell you what --
> because you said it yourself -- part of
> this is definitely madness, right?

EXT. NEW YORK STREET #3 -- NIGHT

ARTHUR walking. VERNE somewhere back there --

> MICHAEL (PHONE/OVER)
> ...There's a chemical part of this,
> and you know it, and I know it, and if
> you're ready to start with that, then
> I'm more than willing to meet you
> halfway and cop to the fact that, <u>yes</u>,
> the situation sucks. The case sucks.
> U/North sucks. We can start with
> that...

INT. ARTHUR'S LOFT/BATHROOM -- NIGHT

IKER with the medicine cabinet open. There must be forty
prescriptions jammed in here and he's checking every single
one, as he listens to --

> MICHAEL'S VOICE
> (on the answering machine)
> ...You hear me, Arthur? Pick up the
> goddam phone.
> (silence)
> I'm telling you you're right, okay?
> About what we are. I'm saying you're
> crazy -- the behavior's completely out
> of control -- but you're right. You
> called it. We're janitors. Okay?
> <u>I get it</u>...

INT. MICHAEL'S APARTMENT/LIVING ROOM -- NIGHT

> MICHAEL
> ...but we came to this, Arthur, we
> had choices. It didn't just happen
> overnight. You can't just suddenly
> say, "Hey, sorry. Game over. I'm
> into miracles now."
> (suddenly)
> Goddamit, Arthur, pick up the fucking
> phone and talk to me! Whatever the
> hell else you think is so important
> right now, you better let me help you
> on this, because I'm telling you
> straight up here, janitor to janitor,
> I don't see anybody else with a broom
> on the horizon.
> (one last hopeful pause,
> before, "<u>beep</u>"--)

> MACHINE VOICE
> "The answering disc is currently full.
> Please try your call again later."

MICHAEL left hanging. He puts down the phone. Drains his
wine glass. Stands at the window.

EXT. TIMES SQUARE -- NIGHT

ARTHUR walking through the neon canyon. Bathing in the
miracle of it all. His eyes seem locked open, gathering
stimuli faster than the speed of light. Every moment --
every beatific instant -- has a purpose. Everything is fuel
for the significance turbine spinning inside him. He slows
his pace, hesitates for a moment and --

EXT. ARTHUR'S TIMES SQUARE POV -- NIGHT

DIAMOND VISION BILLBOARD -- a familiar logo --

u/north
we grow your world together

INT. FARMHOUSE KITCHEN -- DAY

Cold, rural Wisconsin. A tired old room in a tired old
house. A WALL PHONE RINGING. BIG SISTER, the Farmer's Wife,
hauling a baby on her hip as she moves to answer it. THE
FARMER and YOUNG DAUGHTER sitting over breakfast in the BG.

                    BIG SISTER
               (grabbing the phone)
          Hello?

                    ARTHUR/PHONE
          Is Anna there?

                    BIG SISTER
          Hang on...
               (calling into the house)
          Where's Anna?
               (continuing, as--)

EXT. TRIBECA STREET -- DAY (CONT)

Same time. A PANEL TRUCK parked here. It's a scuffed-up,
late model vehicle. Some half-assed electrical supply logo
buried beneath the graffiti. About as anonymous as it gets.

                    BIG SISTER (PHONE/OVER)
          "...Anna! Where is she? ANNA!"

INT. THE PANEL TRUCK -- DAY (CONT)

Surprise. Welcome to a perfect mobile, urban surveillance
HQ. Ugly and state-of-the-art. Purely functional. Nothing
Gucci about it. A cot. Tool cases. Cooler. Folding table.

Couple laptops. Space heater. IKER just now clambering in
the back door. VERNE wearing headphones, already plugged in,
waving for him to hurry up --

                    BIG SISTER (PHONE/OVER)
          "-- Anna, you got a phone call!"

VERNE flipping switches, pulling his laptop closer --

INT. FARMHOUSE KITCHEN -- DAY (CONT)

ANNA KYSURSEN grabbing the phone as she comes by, pulling
the cord as far as she can, making sure BIG SISTER is out of
earshot before she answers --

                         ANNA
                    (finally)
               Hello?

                         ARTHUR (PHONE)
               Anna? Hi. It's Arthur...

                         ANNA
               Hey.

                         ARTHUR (PHONE)
               Did you sleep?

                         ANNA
               I guess.

INT. ARTHUR'S LOFT -- DAY (CONT)

ARTHUR pacing with the phone --

                         ARTHUR
               Did you think about what we said?

                         ANNA (PHONE)
               Yeah.

                         ARTHUR
               You didn't tell anybody, did you?

INTERCUTTING NOW -- FARMHOUSE/LOFT

                         ANNA
               No.
                    (eyes to the kitchen)
               My sister's spying on me but that's
               normal.

                    ARTHUR
          Because I meant what I said.

                    ANNA
          I know, it's just there's like four-
          hundred and fifty people in this
          lawsuit, why are you choosing me?

                    ARTHUR
          I don't know. I'm crazy, right?

                    ANNA
              (laughing)
          That's for sure...

                    ARTHUR
          Does it matter, Anna? I mean,
          really? Isn't it? Isn't that what
          you wait for?...

ANNA smiles. No one's ever spoken to her like this before.

                    ARTHUR
          ...To find someone, and they're like
          a lens and suddenly you're looking
          through them and everything's changed.
          Nothing can ever be the same again...
              (he's rattling on, but--)

                    BIG SISTER (OS)
              (sharply, from behind)
          Who're you talking to?

ANNA wheels around. BIG SISTER standing in the pantry door.
Sour look in her eye. Squirming kid on her hip.

                    FARMER
          You're gonna tie up the phone all
          night, we got a right to know.

                    ANNA
          It's for me, okay? I get calls too!

ANNA pulling the phone wire as far as it goes, disappearing
into a back stairwell. Closing the door behind her, as --

INT.   THE PANEL TRUCK -- DAY (CONT)

Silence. VERNE and IKER listening to the continuing
conversation over headphones. AUDIO LIGHTS on the equipment
rising and falling as Arthur and Anna keep talking.

INT.   COFFEE SHOP -- DAY

ZABEL eating breakfast. MICHAEL with just coffee.

                    MICHAEL
          I can get you twelve on Monday.

                    ZABEL
          Twelve is weak. Twelve looks bad.

                    MICHAEL
          How do you figure that?

                    ZABEL
          They look at seventy-five. They look
          at you. They're wondering what the
          problem is. Now you say twelve.
          That's just gonna make people nervous.

                    MICHAEL
          Gabe, this was the day before
          yesterday, okay? Let me get my ducks
          in a row here.

                    ZABEL
          What's the car worth?

                    MICHAEL
          It's a lease. It's the firm's.

                    ZABEL
          So go to the bank. You got the
          apartment. You refinance.

                    MICHAEL
          I did that three months ago.

Big news. A nasty pause. ZABEL with the polygraph stare.

                    ZABEL
          You back at the tables?

                    MICHAEL
          Oh yeah, like I need the action.
          I don't have enough going on.
               (the very idea)
          I hope you're kidding.

                    ZABEL
          He finds out you're playing cards
          with his money. There's no dialogue
          after that.

                    MICHAEL
         So much for Old Time's Sake, huh?

                    ZABEL
         Do everyone a favor. Get out the
         treasure map and start digging.
         You got a week.

ZABEL goes back to his eggs. MICHAEL walks.

INT. MARTY BACH'S TOWNHOUSE/FOYER -- DAY

CINDY BACH leading MICHAEL in from the foyer. She's late
thirties. Pure trophy. Blonde, horsey, peppy.

                    CINDY
              (walk and talk)
         He's been on the phone all morning.
         What else is new, right?

TWO SIX-YEAR OLDS running wild in the background --

                    CINDY
         Jamie! No running in the kitchen!
              (calling to some unseen
               babysitter--)
         Soroya! Are you watching them?
              (back to Michael)
         He's upstairs, he's taken over the
         living room...
              (pointing the way)
         Go for it. <u>Soroya</u>!
              (kids getting wilder in
               the background now--)
         Don't you just love Saturday morning?

INT. TOWNHOUSE LIVING ROOM -- DAY

The grand parlor floor. Everything perfect except for the
TWO DOZEN DOCUMENT BOXES piled around the room. On the side
of each box, the word EDENS and a number. MARTY poring over
paperwork.

                    MICHAEL
         Marty...

MARTY turns back. Focuses.

                    MARTY
         You know what he's doing? He's making
         their case...
              (the boxes)
         I'm going through his files, I'm
                    (MORE)

MARTY (cont'd)
          reading this...he's building a case
          against U/North.

                    MICHAEL
          No one's gonna let him do that.

                    MARTY
          Let him?
               (furious)
          Who's gonna stop him? You know what
          I just heard? He's calling these
          plaintiffs now -- this woman from
          the deposition? -- he's calling
          these people -- he's got these
          discovery documents stashed away
          here...
               (he's stunned)
          It's a fucking nightmare. I've been
          trying him all morning, you can't even
          leave a message, he's got the whole
          machine jammed up.

MICHAEL watching him pull another bunch of files from a box.

                    MICHAEL
               (something on the floor)
          Is that his briefcase?

                    MARTY
          Yeah. Why?

                    MICHAEL
          We've been looking for it.

                    MARTY
          I don't know. It came up with all
          the stuff from his office.
               (lying effortlessly)
          You can't believe the crap he's got
          stashed away in here.

MICHAEL nods. Accepting this. Plus there's another agenda
he'd like to get to here.

                    MICHAEL
          So, Marty, look, I'm kind of in a
          spot here.
               (Marty focuses)
          I need a loan. I need eighty grand.

MARTY hesitates.

                    MARTY
          I thought you were done with all that.

                    MICHAEL
It's not the cards. Nothing like that.
It's the restaurant.

                    MARTY
Eighty thousand?

                    MICHAEL
I didn't mean to jump you like this.
I've been trying to get a meeting with
you alone now for two weeks.
        (just going for it)
And I know about the merger. Whether
I'm supposed to know or not.

                    MARTY
Nothing's final.

                    MICHAEL
That's why I'm asking now. You're
my meal ticket, Marty. I mean, let's
face it, once this is out of your
hands, I'm screwed. You'll be cashed
out and I'll be staring at Barry and
a bunch of strangers trying to
explain what the hell it is I do.

                    MARTY
Everybody knows how valuable you are,
Michael. Everybody who needs to know.

                    MICHAEL
I'm forty-five. I'm broke. I've been
riding shotgun for twelve years and I
still don't have any equity. Excuse me
if I don't feel reassured.

                    MARTY
Nobody told you to go into the bar
business.

                    MICHAEL
I only opened the place so I'd have a
way out.

                    MARTY
I had no idea you were so unhappy.

                    MICHAEL
C'mon, Marty...
        (pushing down his temper)
How many times have I asked you to
let me get back on a litigation team.
How many times?

MARTY
Anybody can go to court. You think
that's so special?

MICHAEL
I was good at it.

MARTY
So what? So are a lot of people.
At <u>this</u> -- what you do -- at this,
you're great. For crissake, Michael,
you have what everybody wants; you
have a niche. You made a place, you
made this niche for yourself. And if
it's nostalgia -- "Oh, you should've
seen me when I was a D.A. back in
Queens." -- then let me give you a
serious piece of advice: Leave it
there. God forbid you're not as
good as you remember. Because I've
seen that happen too.

MICHAEL
But I didn't come for advice, did I?

MARTY
So this is what? Quid pro quo?

MICHAEL
What do you mean?

MARTY
I give you the loan or you don't help
out with Arthur?

MICHAEL
I never said that.

MARTY
Maybe you should. Because <u>this</u>...
     (Arthur's papers)
This is cancer. This is something we
don't get it reined-in and cleaned up
soon, everything's vulnerable.
<u>Everything</u>.

MICHAEL
What're you telling me?

MARTY
That I'm counting on you.
     (the grand gesture)
I'm telling you that by this time
next week Arthur will be under control
               (MORE)

                              MARTY   (cont'd)
                    and everyone who needs to, will have
                    been reminded of your infinite value.

                              MICHAEL
                    Jesus, Marty...

MARTY suddenly smiling. Good cheer blossoming.

                              MARTY
                    When the fuck did you get so
                    delicate?

MICHAEL left hanging, no chance to respond, because here come
THE KIDS -- running up the stairs -- SQUEALING AND SCREAMING
-- chasing each other into the room and --

                              MARTY
                    -- there you are! --
                       (making a playful grab--)
                    -- into the lion's den! -- gotcha! --

MICHAEL standing there rocked, as MARTY starts roaring at
the kids and they start squealing even louder and --

EXT.   TRIBECA STREET/DOOR TO ARTHUR'S LOFT -- DAY

THE BUILDING DIRECTORY. Five apartments. One per floor.
Five names -- one of them EDENS. Buzzer. Intercom.

MICHAEL pressing the buzzer for the umpteenth time. And
again. And nothing. He tries the door. And it's loose.
But then he stops. Stepping back. Fuck it.

Glancing back up to the third floor windows as he crosses
the street and --

INT.   THE PANEL TRUCK -- DAY

VERNE alone at the console --

                              IKER (RADIO)
                    "-- here comes that guy again -- just
                    passing you now --"

There -- ON ONE OF THE LAPTOPS -- MICHAEL jogging past some
low-res surveillance camera as --

INT.   THE MERCEDES -- DAY

A minute later. HENRY reading as MICHAEL gets back in.

                              HENRY
                    Why don't you just call Uncle Gene
                    and get the cops to help you?

                    MICHAEL
          It's not that kind of problem.

                    HENRY
          How much longer are we doing this?

                    MICHAEL
          I don't know.

EXT. TRIBECA STREETS -- DAY

Half hour later. THE MERCEDES cruising Tribeca.

EXT. TRIBECA STREET -- DAY

Later. THE MERCEDES double parked. MICHAEL walking back
to the car. Another dead-end.

INT. THE MERCEDES -- DAY (CONT)

MICHAEL driving. Scanning. HENRY's patience has thinned.

                    HENRY
          If we're not gonna get to the movies
          why don't you just say so.
               (beat)
          I want to go home.

                    MICHAEL
          Hang on, Henry --
               (something they just
               passed--)

MICHAEL whips the car to the curb --

                    MICHAEL
               (already jumping out--)
          -- stay right here -- lock the doors --
          I'll be right back -- don't move! --

EXT. TRIBECA STREET -- DAY (CONT)

MICHAEL up the sidewalk to the alley --

EXT. ALLEY -- DAY (CONT)

ARTHUR walking away.

                    MICHAEL
               (jogging after him)
          Arthur! Arthur! Wait up!

ARTHUR stops. Turns. Caught. In his arms he's cradling
twenty-five fresh baguettes.

                    ARTHUR
          Whoaa...
               (almost losing his
                loaves--)
          Michael. Jesus. You scared me.

                    MICHAEL
          Making a delivery?

                    ARTHUR
          No...
               (smiling)
          Very funny. Nothing like that...
               (as if it were all
                completely natural
                and needed no further
                explanation--)
          Have one...go on...really...
               (offering)
          It's still warm. Best bread I've
          ever had in my life.

MICHAEL suddenly holding warm French bread.

                    MICHAEL
          So welcome home.

                    ARTHUR
          I know. The hotel. I'm sorry.
          I was getting a little overwhelmed.

                    MICHAEL
          But you're feeling better now?

                    ARTHUR
          Yes. Definitely. Much better.

                    MICHAEL
          Just not enough to call me back.

ARTHUR hesitant. Straining to keep the mania down.

                    ARTHUR
          I wanted to organize my thoughts.
          Before I called. That's what I've
          been doing.

                    MICHAEL
          And how's that going?

                    ARTHUR
          Good. Very good. I just...
               (fighting the flood)
          I need to be more precise. That's
                    (MORE)

                    ARTHUR (cont'd)
my goal.
     (he smiles)
Speak softly and carry a big baguette.

There's a beat. Their history rushing in around them.

                    MICHAEL
As good as this feels, you know where
it goes.

                    ARTHUR
No. You're wrong. What feels so good
is not knowing where it goes.

                    MICHAEL
How do I talk to you, Arthur? So you
hear me? Like a child? Like a nut?
Like everything's fine? What's the
secret? Because I need you to hear me.

                    ARTHUR
I hear everything.

                    MICHAEL
Then hear this: <u>You need help.</u>
Before this gets too far, you need
help. You've got great cards here.
You keep your clothes on, you can
pretty much do any goddamn thing you
want. You want out? You're out.
You wanna bake bread? Go with God.
There's one wrong answer in the whole
pile and there you are with your arms
around it.

                    ARTHUR
I said I was sorry.

                    MICHAEL
You thought the hotel was overwhelming?
You keep pissing on this case, they're
gonna cut you off at the knees.

                    ARTHUR
I don't know what you're talking about.

                    MICHAEL
I'm out there trying to cover for you!
I'm telling people everything's fine,
you're gonna be fine, everything's
cool. I'm out there running this Price-
Of-Genius speech for anybody who'll
listen and I get up this morning and I
find out you're calling this girl in
                    (MORE)

                    MICHAEL   (cont'd)
Wisconsin and you're messing with
documents and God knows what else and --

                    ARTHUR
How can you know that?

                    MICHAEL
-- they'll take everything -- your
partnership, the equity --

                    ARTHUR
How do you know who I call?

                    MICHAEL
-- they'll pull your license!

                    ARTHUR
HOW DO YOU KNOW I CALLED ANNA?

                    MICHAEL
From Marty! You're denying it?

                    ARTHUR
How does he know?

                    MICHAEL
I don't know. I don't give a shit.

ARTHUR stepping back. Flushed. Paranoia rising.

                    ARTHUR
You're tapping my phones.

                    MICHAEL
     (it's to weep)
Jesus, Arthur...

                    ARTHUR
Explain it! Explain how Marty knows.

                    MICHAEL
You chased this girl through a parking
lot with your dick hanging out! You
don't think she got off the phone with
you and speed-dialed her lawyer?

                    ARTHUR
She wouldn't do that. I know that.

                    MICHAEL
Really. You think your judgement is
state-of-the-art right now?
     (before he can step away)
They're putting everything on the table
                    (MORE)

MICHAEL (cont'd)
here. You need to stop and think this
through. I will help you think this
through. I will find someone to help
you think his through. Don't do this.
You're gonna make it easy for them.

ARTHUR draws himself up. We saw a glimpse of this in
Milwaukee. The teeth. The shark beneath the breadloaves.

ARTHUR
I have great affection for you,
Michael, and you lead a very rich and
interesting life, but you're a bagman
not an attorney. If your intention
was to have me committed, you should've
kept me in Wisconsin where the arrest
record, videotape, and eyewitness
accounts of my inappropriate behavior
had jurisdictional relevance. I have
no criminal record in the State of
New York and the crucial determining
criteria for involuntary commitment
is danger: "Is the defendant a danger
to himself or others." You think
you've got the horses for that? Good
luck and God bless. But I'll tell
you this, the last place you want to
see me is in court.

ARTHUR muscles up his bread. He's leaving.

MICHAEL
I'm not the enemy.

ARTHUR
Then who are you?

And he's walking. MICHAEL almost calling after him. Then
not. Then nothing. Standing on the sidewalk with a baguette
in his hand and a great variety of failures arranging
themselves around his heart.

EXT. HILTON HOTEL GYM -- NIGHT

A glass box. Like an aquarium from this distance. It's
empty this late, one lonely runner pounding a treadmill.
As MUSIC -- this catchy, electronic pulsing theme -- starts
playing, and if it sounds a little like a jingle, that's
okay, because it is --

CHORAL VOICES
"...we grow your world together...we
grow your world together...we grow
your world together..."

And then, just as THE MUSIC starts to fade out, it begins
again from the top, CONTINUING AGAIN, as we --

INT. NEW YORK HILTON GYM -- NIGHT

It's KAREN on the treadmill. Running in place. And THE
MUSIC, that electronic pulse, RISING and FALLING and --

> CHORAL VOICES
> *"...we grow your world together...we*
> *grow your world together..."*
> (over and over, as we--)

INT. MICHAEL'S APARTMENT/LIVING ROOM -- NIGHT

HENRY teaching MICHAEL how to play Realm and Conquest --
the game version of the story Henry's been talking about.
PLAYING CARDS spread across a glass table. Each card a
portrait -- ORCS, MAGES, RIVERWYNDERS, etc. -- complete with
descriptions, numbers, code-colors, etc. And THE U/NORTH
JINGLE just bubbling along in the BG, as --

> CHORAL VOICES
> *"...we grow your world together...we*
> *grow your world together..."*
> (starting over, as we--)

INT. THE PANEL TRUCK -- NIGHT

VERNE and IKER at the console listening over headphones.

> IKER
> What the hell is he doing?

> VERNE
> We should've put a camera in there.

INT. ARTHUR'S LOFT -- NIGHT

A TELEVISION SCREEN. A U/NORTH COMMERCIAL. One of those
huge, ambiguous, corporate feel-good spots. THE MUSIC
playing over a series of comforting utopian images --

> CHORAL VOICES
> *"...we grow your world together...we*
> *grow your world together..."*

Except this time it finishes. Image freezing. <u>Silence</u>.

ARTHUR standing in the middle of the room. He's got two
remote controls in his hand. One goes to the VCR where he's
just frozen the U/NORTH COMMERCIAL in it's final frame, the
other controls the cassette deck on the stereo. He's
replaying the video over and over to make an audio loop of

the U/North theme music. ZAP -- he's rewinding the VCR.
ZAP -- he's pausing the cassette deck. ZAP -- he stopping
the VCR. ZAP -- he's hitting "record" and --

INT.   HILTON HOTEL HALLWAY -- NIGHT

KAREN leaving the gym. Sweaty. Arms loaded with paperwork.
Trudging toward the elevators. As THE U/NORTH MUSIC STARTS
AGAIN, except now, we also hear:

                    ARTHUR (V.O.)
               Here it is. Covered in sequins.
               A hidden gem, rescued from the
               vaults...
                    (continuing, as--)

INT.   ARTHUR'S LOFT -- NIGHT

ARTHUR in mid-broadcast. Talking into the receiver of his
phone as if it he were a DJ in the midst of a broadcast. In
his hand, U/NORTH MEMO #229. And as the pre-recorded U/NORTH
MUSIC blasts from the stereo --

                    ARTHUR
               ...One of our all time favorites --
               an underground hit that we think is
               finally ready for it's day in the
               sunshine. Without further ado...
               United-Northfield's Culcitate Internal
               Research Memorandum #229....

INT.   MICHAEL'S APARTMENT/LIVING ROOM -- NIGHT

HENRY crashed on the couch. MICHAEL watching his son sleep.

                    ARTHUR (V.O.)
                    (reading it)
               ...*Conclusion*. *The unanticipated*
               market growth for Culcitate by small
               farms in colder climates demands
               further cost-benefit analysis.
               In-house field studies have indicated
               the possibility that smaller, short-
               season farms with poor drainage,
               dependent on well-water for human
               consumption are at risk for potentially
               toxic particulate concentrations...

INT.   THE PANEL TRUCK -- NIGHT

Emergency. Arthur's reading of the memo has spiked the
urgency level in here by a thousand percent. IKER working
the console. VERNE speed-dialing a cell phone, as --

>   ARTHUR (V.O.)
>   *...Culcitate's great market*
>   *advantage, that it is tasteless,*
>   *colorless and does not precipitate,*
>   *has the potential to mask and*
>   *intensify any possible exposures.*
>   *Further studies and cost/benefit*
>   *analyses need to concentrate in these*
>   *critical follow-up areas....*

INT. KAREN'S HILTON HOTEL ROOM -- NIGHT

THE PHONE RINGING as the door opens. KAREN juggling her
paperwork and sweat clothes, rushing to grab it, as we hear --

>   ARTHUR (V.O.)
>   *...Chemical modification of the*
>   *Culcitate product -- the addition of*
>   *a detector molecule, such as an*
>   *odorant or colorant -- would require*
>   *a top down retooling of the Culcitate*
>   *manufacturing process...*

EXT. SIXTH AVENUE -- NIGHT

Empty midnight. KAREN wearing sweat clothes beneath a coat.
Clutching a pair of headphones to her ears, listening to --

>   ARTHUR (V.O.)
>   *...These cost while assumed to be*
>   *significant were not the subject of*
>   *the study summarized here..*

VERNE standing beside her. It's his Walkman. He brought the
tape. Waiting for her to finish listening.

>   ARTHUR (V.O.)
>   *...Clearly the release of these*
>   *internal research documents would*
>   *compromise the effective marketing of*
>   *Culcitate and must be kept within the*
>   *protective confines of United*
>   *Northfield's secret language.*

And it's done. KAREN takes off the headphones. Hands them
back to VERNE. She's dazed. She looks ill.

>   VERNE
>   It seemed to warrant...

>   KAREN
>   Yes.

An awkward beat. People, cars...life going by.

                    KAREN
          This just...whatever you do...you
          have to contain this.

                    VERNE
          Contain?

                    KAREN
          Right. That's my question. Short
          of, whatever else...something more.
          What's the option for something along
          those lines?

                    VERNE
          You're talking about paper? The data?

                    KAREN
          That there's a more limited option,
          is what I'm asking...
               (cold sweat fumbling)
          Something I'm not thinking of.

                    VERNE
          We deal in absolutes.

                    KAREN
          Okay. I understand. I do.

                    VERNE
          The materials, I'm not a lawyer, we
          try. We do what we can.

                    KAREN
          And the other way?

                    VERNE
          Is the other way.

Heavy pause. Life passing all around them.

                    KAREN
          But you think it's doable.

                    VERNE
          We have some good ideas. You say
          move, we move. The moment our ideas
          don't look so good, we back off and
          reassess.

                    KAREN
          Okay.

                         VERNE
          You mean okay, you understand?
          Or okay, proceed?
               (silence)
          Maybe you want to bring Don in on it.

                         KAREN
          No.
               (on that she's sure)
          Don's not in this. He's busy. It's
          got nothing to do with Don.

VERNE nods. But hanging. Where are they? Still waiting for
an answer, as --

EXT. SUBDIVISION RANCH HOUSE -- DAY

Just another half-acre in an ageing 60's housing development.
THE MERCEDES parked in the driveway.

                    A DOZEN VOICES (OVER)
          Happy Birthday to you. Happy birthday
          to you. Happy birthday dear, Pappy...
               (continuing, as we--)

INT. RANCH HOUSE/DINING ROOM -- DAY

A cop's house. MICHAEL, HENRY and a dozen members of the
Clayton tribe, singing to RAYMOND, 75, the withered, widower,
patriarch of this clan.

                    A DOZEN VOICES
          ...happy Birthday to you!!!

STEPHANIE, Michael's older sister carrying the cake. She
lives next door with three teenage kids, KAY, MARK and EAMON.
Her husband, NORMAN, a simple guy who owns a bakery route.

                         STEPHANIE
          Go on dad, make a wish...

                         RAYMOND
          I get what I wish for, it'll kill me.

This gets a laugh. GENE, Michael's younger brother, is a
Major Case Detective in Queens. His wife is MICHELLE. He's
got two sons in tow, GREG, 16; EDDIE, 12. Grumpy jocks.

                         GENE
          I don't know, Pap, if you're still
          wishing for it, you got a fighting
          chance.

RAYMOND smiles. Sends an emphysemic puff toward the candle.
Doesn't quite get it. STEPHANIE to the rescue. So the
candle's out. And now it's pass-the-plates, and who's having
coffee, and how-do-you-like-it?, and Stephanie you're a saint
for baking from scratch...

> MICHELLE
> (to husband Gene)
> You have time for cake?

> GENE
> I'll take one to go.

> STEPHANIE
> Henry, honey...
> (handing him the slice
> to pass--)
> ...can you?...that's for Uncle Gene.

HENRY handing GENE his cake to go and --

> MICHAEL
> You're going in?

> GENE
> I'm late already.

> MICHAEL
> Shit...

> MICHELLE
> (catching this)
> You're not both running out.

> MICHAEL
> I got a situation...

> GENE
> What? You can't hang?

> MICHAEL
> *You're* going in.

> GENE
> I've got a shift.

> MICHAEL
> Yeah, well so do I.

> GENE
> C'mon man, you haven't been up here
> in months. Henry hasn't seen the
> boys, I don't even know when...
> (MORE)

                    GENE (cont'd)
          (quieter)
     Just stay for an hour, the girls
     did all this stuff, he'll be asleep
     by then. Walk me out...

INT. RANCH HOUSE/PLAYROOM --DAY

Minute later. Downstairs off the garage. GENE putting on a
tie. Badge. Gun. As --

                    GENE
     Timmy's been calling me.
     He's afraid to talk to you.

                    MICHAEL
     He should be.

                    GENE
     It closed out bad, right?

                    MICHAEL
     Is that what he told you?

                    GENE
     The kids are freaking out...his
     in-laws are freaking out...Linda
     can't stop crying long enough to
     start freaking out...

                    MICHAEL
     Hey, she took him back...

                    GENE
     So what? Fuck her and the kids?

                    MICHAEL
     No, fuck Timmy.
          (worked up now)
     And nothing's closed, okay? I sold
     everything but the walls and we're
     still short. So don't talk to me
     about Pam and the kids. I've got my
     hands full. If it was you, he'd be
     in traction.

                    GENE
     He's sick. It's a sickness.

                    MICHAEL
     There's a fresh perspective.

                    GENE
     I've seen a lot of people fall off
     the wagon lately. It's going around.

                         MICHAEL
              Is that pointed at me?

                         GENE
              When do I see you? How do I know
              what you're up to?

                         MICHAEL
              I haven't bet a game in over a year.
              I haven't been in card room in ten
              months.

                         GENE
              Okay...

                         MICHAEL
              I gambled on the bar. I bet on
              Timmy and he wiped me out. That was
              my big play, okay? I put up my
              walk-away money and it's gone and
              I'm scrambling.

                         GENE
              Okay... Cool down. I hear you.
                   (beat)
              I'd be pissed off too.
                   (beat)
              Just hang for an hour, okay?

MICHAEL nods. GENE already checking his watch. Brothers.
Say no more. The everbroken truce.

INT. ARTHUR'S LOFT -- DAY

ARTHUR heading out -- pulling on his coat -- heading for the
door -- checking for keys -- there -- grabbing them off the
side table, as he opens the door and --

ZZZIIPPP!!!!!

A TASER -- 25,000 volts -- from nowhere -- ARTHUR'S BODY
clenching as it hits and --

WE'RE INTO ONE CONTINUOUS SHOT NOW

VERNE and IKER -- already flooding in -- gloves -- hairnets --
surgical boots -- like machines --

IKER -- the athlete -- perfect -- hands catching ARTHUR'S
WRITHING BODY before it hits the floor and --

VERNE -- attack -- gloved hand thrusting down and --

ARTHUR'S FACE -- AEROSOL CAN -- VERNE'S HAND -- two quick
bursts -- point blank -- words -- throat -- everything choked
off -- eyes rolling and --

IKER -- the body drops -- ready for the dead weight and --

VERNE -- kicking shut the door -- back to the body and --

> IKER
> Ready and...

> VERNE
> Lift.

ARTHUR -- like a prop -- limp -- effortless -- IKER and VERNE
flying him through the space -- this horrifying freight train
pas de trois -- and so far this whole thing as taken *eighteen
seconds* --

Heading like a freight train for --

THE LOFT BATHROOM -- here they come -- IKER walking backward
holding ARTHUR'S SHOULDERS -- VERNE guiding him --

> VERNE
> Ready and...turn.

IKER shifting -- they're in -- *twenty six seconds* --

> IKER
> The coat.

> VERNE
> Hold him.

VERNE works off Arthur's coat -- tossing it --

> IKER
> Let me just...

> VERNE
> Ready and...

> IKER
> Down.

ARTHUR sprawled across the bathroom floor and --

> VERNE
> (checking his watch)
> We're good. Prep it.

IKER -- like a shot -- unlacing one of Arthur's boots and --

VERNE -- backpack off -- digging through it -- coming up
with -- A PREPPED SYRINGE and --

IKER -- pulling off Arthur's sock and --

THE MEDICINE CABINET -- <u>flying open</u> -- VERNE searching --
knowing right where to look -- bingo -- BOTTLE -- BOTTLE --
BOTTLE -- pulling them down and --

IKER -- foot is bare -- reaching up -- *forty-one seconds* --

                    IKER
      Bag, I need the wipe...

VERNE -- tossing the backpack -- scanning the pill bottles --

IKER -- coming out of the backpack with a pint of vodka and a
sterile handkerchief and -- *forty-nine seconds* --

VERNE -- stripping open the syringe -- kneeling now and --

ARTHUR'S FACE -- gasping back to life -- he's coming to --
gagging now as IKER wipes the aerosol residue away from his
mouth -- eyes twitching, as they start to open and --

                    IKER
      Better hit it.

ARTHUR'S BARE FOOT -- THE SYRINGE -- up -- in -- between the
toes and --

VERNE -- as he plunges it home -- no hate -- no fear -- no
pleasure -- nothing -- *sixty-seven seconds* and --

ARTHUR'S FACE -- as the eyes open -- just an instant --
catching the light -- these strange masked faces -- then gone
-- just like that -- rolling away -- a little sigh -- a puff
of air -- tongue thickening -- and then still and --

                    IKER
    We good?

                   VERNE
      (checking the pulse)
    Hang on...

                    IKER
    I'm gonna get the shoe back on.

                   VERNE
    We're good.

And it's over. *Ninety seconds start to finish.*

INT.   RANCH HOUSE/LIVING ROOM -- DAY

RANCH HOUSE LIVING ROOM.   Early evening.   Sunday television
torpor.   RAYMOND asleep in his chair.   COUSINS watching a
college basketball game.

CAMERA FINDS

MICHAEL and HENRY getting ready to leave.   STEPHANIE and
MICHELLE hovering --

                    STEPHANIE
               (card in hand)
          That's his number.   Dr. Moolian, see
          if you have any more luck --

                    MICHAEL
          -- okay, let me get into it --

                    STEPHANIE
          -- cause Medicaid, they've just been
          running us in circles with this.

                    MICHELLE
          Let him go, Steph, he's got a date.

                    MICHAEL
          Yeah, with a maniac attorney.

                    STEPHANIE
          Take a night off.   You look tired.

                    MICHAEL
          One of these days...
               (a kiss for each of them,
               as we cut to--

EXT. RANCH HOUSE DRIVEWAY -- DAY

Two minutes later.   MICHAEL and HENRY walking down to the
MERCEDES.   Coming around the car, when --

                    HENRY
          Uncle Timmy?

MICHAEL turns and --

                    TIMMY
          How you doing, Hen?

TIMMY standing there.   Michael's brother.   A big guy that's
been hollowed out by too much of everything.   His bartender
smile, a phony tic he can't quite control anymore.

STILLS

George Clooney as Michael Clayton

Tom Wilkinson as Arthur Edens

Tilda Swinton as Karen Crowder

Sydney Pollack as Marty Bach

Austin Williams as Henry Clayton

Karen Crowder (Tilda Swinton) nervously preparing for her interview at U/North in Omaha.

Karen Crowder, senior in-house counsel for U/North, with her boss, Don Jeffries (Ken Howard).

In a Milwaukee hotel suite, Todd (Matthew Detmer) and Maude (Rachel Black), Karen Crowder's assistants, show her the evidence of the strange behavior of lead litigator Arthur Edens during the deposition.

Karen Crowder (Swinton) strategizing how to prevent further damage to the case.

Michael Clayton (George Clooney) confronting Arthur Edens (Tom Wilkinson) in the holding cell in Milwaukee.

Michael Clayton (Clooney) arranging for the release of Edens (Wilkinson).

Michael Clayton (Clooney) thanking Police Lt. Elston (Christopher Mann) for his help.

Medicated Arthur Edens (Wilkinson) on the phone with Henry Clayton in the Milwaukee hotel.

Henry Clayton (Austin Williams) on the phone in his loft bed in New York City, describing the book *Realm & Conquest* to Arthur Edens.

Anny Kyrsursen (Meritt Wever) discussing the lawsuit with Arthur.

Arthur Edens (Wilkinson) talking from his loft in Tribeca in New York City.

(left to right) Mr. Verne (Robert Prescott) and his associate, Mr. Iker (Terry Serpico), setting up surveillance on Arthur.

Euphoric Arthur Edens (Wilkinson) wandering the streets of New York City, followed by Mr. Verne (Prescott).

(Top and middle) Michael Clayton (Clooney) in an alley in Tribeca finally catching up to Arthur Edens (Wilkinson), cradling a bundle of baguettes as he explains his actions.

Hugging his son, Henry (Williams), Michael Clayton (Clooney) tries to figure out how to help Arthur.

(left to right) Detective Gene Clayton (Sean Cullen), Michael's older brother, and Michael Clayton (Clooney) at their father's birthday party.

Michael Clayton (Clooney) with Gene's wife, Michelle (Susan Egbert).

Timmy Clayton (David Lansbury), Michael's brother and former partner.

Michael (Clooney) and Henry Clayton (Williams) surprised to see Timmy Clayton.

Mr. Verne (Prescott) and Karen Crowder (Swinton) discussing some serious options.

Michael Clayton (Clooney) and law firm head Marty Bach (Sydney Pollack) lamenting Arthur's demise at a New York bar.

In the law offices, Marty Bach (Pollack) settling with Michael Clayton (Clooney), shown holding his check and the critical red-covered memo.

Karen Crowder (Swinton) learning that Michael Clayton has the damaging memo as she faces another grave decision.

Mr. Iver (Serpico) and Mr. Verne (Prescott) in deadly pursuit of Michael Clayton.

Michael Clayton (Clooney) losing the moment of quiet with the horses on the hill after his Mercedes explodes.

Michael Clayton (Clooney) running for his life.

Michael Clayton (Clooney) is rescued by Timmy (Lansbury) at the mall.

Karen Crowder (Swinton) being photographed by Michael Clayton (Clooney) after making her incriminating deal.

Gene Clayton (Cullen) saying goodbye to his brother Michael (Clooney) following the sting operation.

(left to right, foreground) Director/Writer Tony Gilroy with George Clooney on set.

(left to right) Director of Photography Robert Elswit, Producer Jennifer Fox, Director/Writer Tony Gilroy

                         MICHAEL
                Get in the car, Henry.

HENRY hesitates.   Then moving quickly to get into the car.

                         TIMMY
                    (before the door closes)
                Good to see you, Henry.

                         MICHAEL
                What do you want?

                         TIMMY
                I've been sober eight days. I'm back
                at the meetings. I wanted you to know.

                         MICHAEL
                In front of the kid?

                         TIMMY
                Mikey, please, I know how bad I did.
                I swear. I don't know how to make it
                right, but it's all I think about.
                    (he's breaking)
                What can I do? Tell me what to do.

MICHAEL getting in the car. Brick wall.

                         MICHAEL
                Get Stephanie her tires back.

The car door slams shut. TIMMY folding. The shitty stoic
tears of a wounded drunk.

INT.   THE MERCEDES -- DAY (CONT)

MICHAEL puts the car in gear. HENRY quiet as they pull away.

                         HENRY
                Is he crying?

                         MICHAEL
                    (tight)
                I don't know.

                         HENRY
                Because of drugs, right?

                         MICHAEL
                That and everything else.

They drive in silence down the hill. MICHAEL focused on
the road, trying to settle. Then he looks over, just now
realizing how upset the boy really is and --

> HENRY
> (as the car stops)
> What?

> MICHAEL
> Uncle Timmy -- and I mean this -- on
> his best day, he was never as tough
> as you. And I'm not talking about
> crying or the drugs. I'm talking about
> in his heart. You understand me?

HENRY caught in the focus of his father's sudden sincerity.

> HENRY
> Okay.

> MICHAEL
> *Big Tim...Uncle Boss*...all his charming
> bullshit. And I know you love him.
> And I know why. But when you see him
> like this, you don't have to be afraid,
> because that's not how it's gonna be
> for you. You're not gonna be one of
> those people who goes through life
> wondering why things keep falling out
> of the sky around them. You have some
> real steel in you Henry. Inside.
> I see it every time I look at you.
> I see it right now.
> (he tries to smile)
> I don't know where the hell you got it
> from, but you got it.

HENRY silent. Trying to get that down. As A CELL PHONE
begins ringing. The moment broken as MICHAEL starts digging
into his coat pockets and --

> MICHAEL
> (answering)
> Hello...

And there's this just godawful pause. MICHAEL listening to
some really bad news, as we --

EXT. FOURTH PRECINCT STATION HOUSE -- NIGHT

Est. Shot. Cops coming and going, as we hear:

                    DET. DALBERTO (V.O.)
          ...the neighbors came by, they're
          renovating the loft downstairs, they
          had water flooding down from his
          bathroom into their place...

INT.   SIXTH PRECINCT SQUADROOM -- NIGHT

DETECTIVE DALBERTO at his desk. Friendly. Sympathetic.
MICHAEL sitting there. Seriously shaken.

                    DET. DALBERTO
          ...his front door, fire escape, he had
          everything locked up pretty good. It
          took our guys ten minutes, they had to
          break the thing down. He had the
          perimeter alarm set. Pills all over
          the place. So just the scene alone,
          it's pretty definitive for suicide.
          Then I spoke to some of your partners,
          they ran down these problems he'd been
          having lately, so...

                    MICHAEL
          Was there a note?

                    DET. DALBERTO
          No. They looked. There was paperwork
          all over the place -- walls and shit --
          he had stuff up all over. But no note.
          Could be an accident. Or he was gonna
          write a note and just messed up...

                    MICHAEL
          Can I get in there?

                    DET. DALBERTO
          His place? Not now. It's sealed.
          Once that seal goes up it's frozen.
          We're gonna try and reach his daughter,
          I guess, she's off in Europe, she's
          gotta come in, or the ME's gotta come
          back with a toxicology report. That's
          a couple weeks at least it's gotta stay
          like that. They bagged up, you know
          whatever valuables they saw, but...
                  (beat)
          Sorry.

                    MICHAEL
          Sure.

                    DET. DALBERTO
          I know your brother a little. My wife
          works in the one-sixteen out in Queens.

                    MICHAEL
          I'll tell him hello.

                    DET. DALBERTO
          Something comes in, I'll get back to
          you.

                    MICHAEL
          I appreciate it.

                    DET. DALBERTO
          Sorry for your loss.

MICHAEL nods. Stands. End of story.

EXT. NEW YORK BAR -- NIGHT

BARRY pacing on a cell phone outside. He sees MICHAEL
approaching and --

                    BARRY
               (into the phone)
          -- hang on -- just hang on --
               (to Michael)
          There you are...

BARRY finds a sad face. Throws out a hand. MICHAEL joins
this little dance of grief.

                    BARRY
          ...we've been waiting for you...
          they're all in there, I'll be in...

MICHAEL nods. Pulls away and --

INT. THE NEW YORK BAR -- NIGHT

Dark. Funky. Somebody's favorite joint. MARTY BACH and
HALF-A-DOZEN OTHER ATTORNEYS clotted at the bar. These guys
all partners at the firm. Everyone dressed in their Sunday
night come-as-you-are tragedy clothes.

MICHAEL moves down the line. A grim, quiet gauntlet of
mumbled hellos and handshakes. MARTY, truly grief-stricken,
half-drunk, shaky as he comes off his stool to gather MICHAEL
into his arms.

                    MARTY
               (as they embrace)
          ...that stupid bastard...

>   MICHAEL
>   ...I know...

>   MARTY
>   ...what a thing...

>   MICHAEL
>   ...makes no sense...I know...I
>   can't believe it...

Finally they separate. Two wounded souls.

>   MARTY
>   I never even got to talk to him.

EXT.   THE NEW YORK BAR -- NIGHT

BARRY still on his phone call --

>   BARRY
>   (pacing and talking--)
>   ...I'm not gonna start negotiating
>   against myself, if he's got a number
>   he likes he's gonna have to back it
>   up. I'm not getting U/North all
>   fired up if he doesn't have his
>   people in line...

INT.   NEW YORK BAR/BOOTH -- NIGHT

Forty-five minutes later. MICHAEL and MARTY alone now.

>   MICHAEL
>   Did I push too hard?

>   MARTY
>   Not a chance.

>   MICHAEL
>   I just couldn't get through to him.

>   MARTY
>   What? You scared him to death?
>   (ridiculous)
>   The man was a bull. Never happen.

>   MICHAEL
>   So why does he fold?

>   MARTY
>   It's got to be an accident. No note?
>   Arthur without a note? Guy couldn't
>   take a piss without leaving a memo.
>   It has to be an accident.

                    MICHAEL
          I don't get that either. One minute
          he's so pumped up he's gonna take on
          the world, twelve hours later he's
          sucking down pills? Why?

                    MARTY
          Why? Because people are fucking
          incomprehensible. Why...
               (waving the idea away)
          You live this long, you're supposed
          to get something out of it. What did
          I get? I'm still horny and vain and
          afraid to die. What do I know about
          anything?
               (he drinks)
          Thirty years I know Arthur. Good
          years. And what I feel right now?
          If I'm honest? I can't even say it
          it's so awful.

                    MICHAEL
          Say it.
               (silence)
          That we caught a lucky break?

MARTY looks over. Hesitates.

                    MARTY
          We did, didn't we?

MICHAEL nods.

                    BARRY (OS)
          Marty?

They turn. BARRY behind them.

                    BARRY
          We need to get up to the office.

                    MARTY
          They accepted?

                    BARRY
          In principle. Don Jeffries wants us
          on the phone in half an hour.
               (including Michael in
                this now--)
          I tried to explain about Arthur.
          They're a little short on sympathy
          at this point.

                    MICHAEL
          Wait a minute. U/North's settling?

                    BARRY
          They think there's a window. They want
          to try.
               (just the messenger)
          It's their show. What're we gonna do?

MICHAEL stunned. Silent.

                    MARTY
          You did what you could, Michael.
          We all did.
               (draining his drink)
          It is what it is.

BARRY helping MARTY off the stool. Holding his coat.

                    BARRY
          You need a ride?

                    MICHAEL
          No. No, I'm okay.

MARTY with a misty wave good night. MICHAEL watching BARRY
navigate the old man out toward the door, as --

INT.   THE FARMHOUSE KITCHEN -- NIGHT

Dark. THE PHONE RINGING. ANNA'S BIG SISTER padding in,
turning on a light and --

                    BIG SISTER
               (answering)
          Hello?

                    MICHAEL (PHONE/OVER)
          I'm looking for Anna Kysersun?

                    BIG SISTER
          Who is this?

EXT.   THE NEW YORK BAR -- NIGHT

MICHAEL on the sidewalk --

                    MICHAEL/PHONE
          My name is Michael Clayton. I'm an
          attorney in New York and I--

                    BIG SISTER/PHONE
          Well you've got some nerve.

                         MICHAEL/PHONE
              Excuse me?

                         BIG SISTER/PHONE
              You get her all the way to New York
              and then leave her at the airport?
              This is not a complicated person!
              This is a girl who's never been farther
              away from home than Milwaukee!

INT.   THE MERCEDES -- NIGHT

MICHAEL driving, as we hear --

                         MICHAEL/PHONE V.O.
              Wait a minute...

                         BIG SISTER/PHONE V.O.
              No -- you wait! -- she's coming home
              tomorrow! -- and when she does, if you
              call here again, I'm warning you --

EXT.   AIRPORT HOTEL/PARKING LOT -- NIGHT

La Guardia in the background. THE MERCEDES pulling in as --

                         MICHAEL/PHONE V.O.
              -- hang -- hang on -- <u>wait</u> -- are you
              saying she's in New York? -- she's in
              New York, right now?

                         BIG SISTER (PHONE/OVER)
                This is a young girl! Do you hear me?

INT.   FORD TAURUS/AIRPORT HOTEL PARKING LOT -- NIGHT

VERNE and IKER watching MICHAEL get out of the Mercedes --

                         IKER
              What the fuck is this?

INT.   AIRPORT HOTEL HALLWAY -- NIGHT

Empty. Quiet. MICHAEL knocking on a door.

                         MICHAEL
              Anna?
                   (knocking harder)
              <u>Anna</u>?

                         ANNA (OS)
                   (through the door)
              Who is it?

                    MICHAEL
          Anna, my name is Michael Clayton.
          I'm a friend of Arthur's.

AS THE DOOR OPENS just a crack. ANNA standing there.
A frightened small town girl in a strange place.

INT.   FORD TAURUS -- NIGHT

VERNE and IKER as they were. In the dark. Not happy.

                    IKER
          What're you thinking?

                    VERNE
          I'll watch the door. Why don't you
          give his car a good once over?

                    IKER
               (as he gets out)
          How do I know I'm not getting home
          tomorrow?

INT.   AIRPORT HOTEL ROOM -- NIGHT

ANNA sitting on the bed. Crying. MICHAEL in the room's
only chair.

                    ANNA
          ...he didn't want to say exactly
          what it was, just that when I got
          here he would pick me up and show
          me and I would see that it was
          something that would win the whole
          case...even this morning I thought,
          okay, if I get to the airport and
          the ticket's not there, then I'll
          know, okay, you're stupid, now you
          can go home...but it was there and
          he paid like eight hundred dollars
          for a first class ticket, so I just,
          I got on the plane, I believed him...

MICHAEL there for her. Probing very gently here.

                    MICHAEL
          You think maybe he was disappointed?
          Let's say he knew that you'd told
          somebody else about all this. You
          think that might've, in some crazy way,
          that he'd be disappointed by that?

                    ANNA
          But I didn't.

              MICHAEL
You must've told somebody.

              ANNA
No. He made me promise.

              MICHAEL
Nobody knew about this? You never
told anybody?

              ANNA
No...
     (new tears welling)
He really was crazy, wasn't he?

MICHAEL without an answer for that. Watching her cry.

EXT. HUNDRED AND SIXTEENTH PRECINCT -- NIGHT

Queens. Midnight. Patrol cars parked outside. Couple cops
changing shifts.

INT. QUEENS PRECINCT STORAGE ROOM -- NIGHT

NYPD ugly. GENE CLAYTON, shirtsleeves and shoulder holster,
tearing through A HUGE OLD FILING CABINET. HANDS pulling
open the drawers. One after the next. Searching through the
clutter of blank forms and department stationery. MICHAEL
waiting by the door.

              GENE
     (finally)
You talking about these?

He's holding a stack of PROTECTIVE CRIME SCENE SEALS.

              MICHAEL
I only need one.

              GENE
You know what this is?

              MICHAEL
Yes.

              GENE
You said a favor. This is more
than a favor.

              MICHAEL
Nobody's gonna know where it came
from.

                         GENE
              Are you that jammed up?

                         MICHAEL
              What're you talking about?

                         GENE
              It's the restaurant, right? One of
              these guys you owe? "Get me a seal."

                         MICHAEL
              Do you really want to know?

GENE hesitates.

                         GENE
              I'm gonna go take a leak. You'll
              probably be gone when I get back.
                   (he tosses the seals
                    onto the table--)
              You know your way out.

MICHAEL stands aside. GENE pushes past him and out the door.
MICHAEL waiting for him to walk away, as --

EXT. TRIBECA STREET/ARTHUR'S BUILDING -- NIGHT

Two a.m. Dark and quiet.

EXT. ARTHUR'S BUILDING/FRONT DOOR -- NIGHT

MICHAEL with a crowbar. Pushing the door to the limits of
the lock. Checking the street. Wedging the crowbar under
the lock. Leaning. Now harder. And pushing, and...

SNAP. He's in.

INT. THE LANDING OUTSIDE ARTHUR'S LOFT -- NIGHT

THE DOOR TO ARTHUR EDEN'S LOFT. It's a mess. The metal
frame is bent and splintered where the cops beat their way
in. The original lock has been destroyed and replaced by
a short length of chain-link held to a padlock that's been
screwed into the wall. A SEAL -- "Crime Scene Do Not Enter"
-- plastered like a big bandaid across the door and frame.

MICHAEL standing there. Listening to the silence. In his
hand, the seal he took from Gene. Framing it -- making sure
he'll be able to replace it perfectly. He will. Now he's
pulling the crowbar and --

INT. ARTHUR'S LOFT -- NIGHT

Dark. And then light, as THE DOOR falls open. MICHAEL at
the threshold. Hesitating. Listening. Nervous. And then he
steps in. Closing the door behind him, as --

EXT. SOMEONE'S POV -- ARTHUR'S WINDOWS -- NIGHT

As a light comes on in Arthur's loft.

INT. THE FORD TAURUS -- NIGHT (CONT)

VERNE and IKER. It's their POV. Two grim faces.

                    IKER
          This just gets better and better.
               (Verne just staring up
                at that window--)
          What're we doing?

VERNE doesn't answer. Checks his watch. Looks back up to
the window. Lots of ugly wheels turning, as --

INT. ARTHUR'S LOFT -- NIGHT

TIME CUTS -- MICHAEL searching -- moving quietly through
the space. He's not really sure what he's looking for, so
everything's important.

-- MICHAEL flipping through stacks of newspapers.

-- MICHAEL checking a pile of photography books.

-- MICHAEL at a wall covered with pictures of farms.

-- MICHAEL staring at the baguettes piled on a chair.

FINALLY TO

INT. ARTHUR'S LOFT/BATHROOM -- NIGHT

MICHAEL at the threshold. Knowing this is where it happened.
Creeped out. Turning away and --

There on the floor. Arthur's coat.

MICHAEL kneeling to pick up the coat. Stopping suddenly.
Something much more interesting there beside it --

"REALM AND CONQUEST" Book One. The red cover.

MICHAEL just stunned. Stalled. Confused.

CLOSE-UP -- THE BOOK as he begins to flip the pages. And
we've never seen the text before. There are illustrations
at the start of every chapter. Line drawings depicting the
dramatic high points of an epic quest. Chapter One: The
Avian Warriors. Chapter Two: Exile of The Deserters.
Chapter Three: Summons To Conquest.

Arthur has clearly read these first three chapters. Whole
passages are underlined. Notes scrawled here and there in
the margins. Pages folded back. And then --

A BOOKMARK falls out. Fluttering down to the floor.

MICHAEL reaches down to pick it up.

CLOSE-UP -- THE BOOKMARK. It's a receipt.

                 "COPY MASTERS -- YOUR ONE STOP FOR COPIES"

MICHAEL staring at the receipt. Then the book. Then the
receipt. Then --

                         VOICE (OS)
                    Freeze! --

MICHAEL -- totally -- completely startled --

                         VOICE (OS)
                    (it's behind him)
               -- right there asshole! -- get your
               hands up! -- now! -- NOW! --

MICHAEL -- okay -- don't shoot -- raise hands --

                         VOICE
                    (coming closer)
               -- what's in your hand? -- drop it! --

                         MICHAEL
               -- it's just -- it's a book! --

                         VOICE
               -- drop it! -- turn around slowly! --
               who else is here? --

MICHAEL drops the book. Turning around slowly as the SOUND
OF A POLICE RADIO begins to rattle and --

TWO YOUNG NERVOUS POLICE OFFICERS -- guns drawn -- coming
from the open door --

                         COP/VOICE
               -- I said, who else is here? --

                    MICHAEL
          -- nobody, I'm alone --

                    COP
               (to his partner)
          -- check in there -- these closets --
               (to Michael)
          You move I'll take your head off!

MICHAEL frozen like that and the TWO NERVOUS COPS circling
around him and POLICE RADIO CHATTER rising and the big stink
of a terrible mistake wafting through the air, as --

INT. SIXTH PRECINCT QUESTIONING ROOM -- EARLY MORNING

MICHAEL alone with a cold cup of coffee. Staring at himself
in the one-way mirror. Waiting. Finally, THE DOOR opens --

                    DET. DALBERTO
          We need the room.

INT. SIXTH PRECINCT HALLWAY -- EARLY MORNING

DALBERTO walking off. MICHAEL emerges from the questioning
room. GENE waiting for him. Absolutely furious. He wants
to scream but can't. Waiting for DALBERTO to disappear --

                    GENE
          So you know, I now owe this scumbag
          and his wife -- who's a total piece
          of shit in my unit -- now I owe them
          my balls for this.

                    MICHAEL
          I'm sorry, Gene. You know I am.

                    GENE
          "Nobody's gonna know it's me."
               (you asshole)
          You know what happens he doesn't bury
          this? That I gave you this thing?

                    MICHAEL
          It's bad.

                    GENE
          I'm eighteen months away from my
          twenty! You just put my pension in
          jeopardy!

                    MICHAEL
          You made your point.

                    GENE
          It's not a point!

                    MICHAEL
          Who called 911?

                    GENE
          What?

                    MICHAEL
          The building's empty. I was quiet.
          I was there maybe six minutes.
          Who called it in? Does that make
          sense to you, that happening like--

GENE grabbing him -- jerking him close --

                    GENE
          This never happened.

MICHAEL hesitates. Nods. Impatient -- he pushes back --
hard -- breaks Gene's grip. Brothers. Toe-to-toe.

                    GENE
          All these cops think you're a lawyer.
          Then you got all these lawyers thinking
          you're some kind of cop. You've got
          everybody fooled, right? Everybody but
          you. You know exactly what you are.

MICHAEL just taking it. GENE backing away. Turning, and now
he's walking... Gone.

EXT.   VILLAGE STREET -- DAY

Morning. NYU Students swarming the sidewalks.

          "COPY MASTERS -- YOUR ONE STOP FOR COPIES!"

INT.   COPY MASTERS -- DAY

Big college operation. MICHAEL at the counter watching
A COPY KID coming from the back with a heavy cardboard box.
Straining it to the counter.

                    COPY KID
          We tried to call like six times, I
          guess your answering machine is messed
          up or something. We took a shot...
               (opening the box)
          We ran out of red covers.
               (handing one over)
          We only had two thousand in stock, so
          the other thousand we did in blue.

MICHAEL doesn't answer because --

IN HIS HAND

A BOOKLET. A bright red plastic cover. The title:

SUMMONS TO CONQUEST

And when he flips it open. There it is, the by-now-familiar
UNITED-NORTHFIELD MEMO #229 in all it's ugly splendor.

MICHAEL reading the memo. Lost in it. As we watch the
realization take shape -- how dangerous...how sensitive...
how threatening these few sheets of paper must be.

>   COPY KID
>   (Michael still reading)
>   It's okay, right?

MICHAEL looks up. Dazed.

>   MICHAEL
>   What? Yeah. It's fine.

>   COPY KID
>   You got a van or...
>   (sensing confusion)
>   There's like ten boxes.

>   MICHAEL
>   Right.
>   (forcing himself to rally
>   here--)
>   Look, I'll tell you what...
>   (finding his wallet)
>   I'll give you fifty bucks to keep
>   the rest till the end of the week.

COPY KID smiles. Sure. MICHAEL grabbing that one box on the
counter. Turning away to exit and --

IKER standing there. Next in line. Watching him go --

EXT. SIXTH AVENUE -- DAY

DON JEFFRIES walking with Karen's two assistants, MAUDE and
TODD and several U/NORTH EXECUTIVES toward the Kenner, Bach &
Ledeen offices. KAREN on a phone call, falling behind --

>   KAREN
>   (calling to the group)
>   Don!
>   (MORE)

>   KAREN (cont'd)
>   (he turns back)
>   You guys go ahead. I'll catch up.

And they do. And KAREN stops there. Turns --

EXT. KAREN'S POV/ACROSS THE PLAZA -- DAY (CONT)

VERNE waiting. Watching her come. Not a happy reunion.

>   KAREN
>   What are you doing here? You were
>   leaving...

>   VERNE
>   Do you know Michael Clayton?

>   KAREN
>   From the... Yes. Why?

>   VERNE
>   We have a situation.

He hands her A RED COVERED BOOKLET. Calmly checking the
perimeter as she opens it and --

INT. LAW FIRM/SENIOR PARTNERS HALLWAY -- DAY

ANOTHER RED BOOKLET. This one in MICHAEL'S HAND. This one
in motion because he's walking and --

WE'RE TRACKING WITH HIM

Power central. Normally it's quiet and subdued up here, but
the combination of Arthur's death the night before and the
sudden paroxysm of activity on the U/North settlement seems
to have drawn a crowd. MICHAEL heading briskly for the
central reception atrium, passing ATTORNEYS and SUPPORT STAFF
clustered along the way. There's A WEEPY GROUP bunched near
Arthur's office and --

>   ATTORNEY #1
>   (as Michael goes by)
>   Did they find you?

>   MICHAEL
>   Who?

>   ATTORNEY #1
>   Marty.
>   (pointing around the
>   corner and--)
>   I don't think they went down yet...

MICHAEL moving around the corner and into --

<u>INT.   SENIOR PARTNER'S RECEPTION AREA -- DAY (CONT)</u>

THIRTY PEOPLE -- ASSOCIATES, SUPPORT PEOPLE, ATTORNEYS --
scrambling over STACKS OF PRESENTATION DOCUMENTS -- this
stuff was supposed to be ready for the U/North meeting and
there's been some sort of clerical fuck up. So now there's
twenty-five opinions on how to fix it and fifteen
conversations going and nine cell phones ringing and six
people on their knees going through the pages and --

                    BARRY
              (on a mobile phone in
               the middle of it all--)
          -- so either we cap the interest on
          the primary trust or somebody figures
          out how to split the custody fees --
              (spotting Michael)
          -- the audit's mandatory, right? --
              (covering the phone,
               calling back over
               his shoulder--)
          -- Marty! --
              (then the phone--)
          -- no, just hang on --
              (then to Michael--)
          -- he's been looking for you --
              (then back to the
               phone, as--)

MICHAEL crosses the chaos to the elevator bank and --

                    MARTY
          Your phone is off. There's too much
          going on for your phone to be off.

                    MICHAEL
          I need a minute.

                    MARTY
              (impatient, tired)
          Yeah well, now we're late, so...

                    MICHAEL
          We never got to finish last night.

                    MARTY
          What'd you do? Close the place?
          You look like hell.

                    MICHAEL
          I left right after you did.

                    MARTY
          If you say so.
               (checking his watch)
          We've been here all night. We had
          to make an announcement.
               (turning now--)
          Jean! Jeannie!
               (calling to his Assistant
                across the way--)
          Where's the thing? The envelope?
               (back to Michael)
          So I wanted your input, but I couldn't
          get you and I had to pull the trigger.
          I put Bob Nast and Kim -- which is
          probably a mistake -- they're gonna try
          to pull together a memorial service by
          the end of the week. I told them to
          call you if they need help, okay?
               (distracted now because
                Jean's holding something
                up for him to see--)
          -- no, no, the other one --
               (back to Michael)
          So we cut a check for you this
          morning, but there's some strings
          attached. And Barry, there's no way
          around it, he's got to be involved.

                    MICHAEL
          What if Arthur was onto something?

                    MARTY
          What do you mean? Onto what?

     MICHAEL hesitating because here's JEAN, tapping her watch for
     MARTY to hurry up as she hands him A SMALL GRAY ENVELOPE --

                    MICHAEL
          U/North. What if Arthur wasn't just
          crazy? What if he was right?

                    MARTY
          Right about what? That we're on
          the wrong side?

                    MICHAEL
          Wrong side. Wrong way. All of it.

                    MARTY
          This is news? We're defending cancer
          for crissake. The case reeked from
          Day One. Fifteen years in, I've got
          to tell you how we pay the rent?

                    MICHAEL
          What would they do, though, if they
          thought Arthur was gonna go public?

                    MARTY
          What would they do? Are you fucking
          soft? They're doing it!
               (honestly incredulous)
          We don't straighten this settlement
          out in the next twenty-four hours,
          they're gonna withhold nine million
          dollars in fees they owe us. Then
          they're gonna pull out the video of
          Arthur's flashdance in Milwaukee and
          sue us for legal malpractice, except
          there won't be anything to win because
          by that point the merger with London
          will be dead and we'll be selling off
          the furniture.
               (handing Michael the
                envelope now--)
          That's eighty. We're calling it a
          bonus. You're getting a three year
          contract at your current numbers.
          That's assuming this all works out.

And now, before MICHAEL can get his footing, here comes --

                    BARRY
               (the envelope)
          You're doing this <u>now</u>?

                    MARTY
               (the documents)
          Are they ready?

                    BARRY
          Almost. They're proofing.
               (to Michael))
          Look, I agreed to this, okay?
          But there's rules now. You want
          the contract, you're signing a
          confidentiality agreement and it's
          gonna be retroactive and it's gonna
          be bulletproof. Because Marty's too
          nice to say it, but with everything
          you know about this place and the
          clients and the people who work here,
          it makes things just a little too
          weird when you come in and ask for
          eighty grand.

A nasty beat. MICHAEL stung. Roiling.

                    MICHAEL
          If I was gonna shake anybody down,
          Barry, I'd come right to you. And it
          wouldn't be for eighty grand.
               (to Marty)
          Is this him or you?

                    BARRY
          Hey, if I'm wrong, I apologize.

                    MICHAEL
          You're wrong. You're way-the-fuck
          wrong.

                    BARRY
          So there you go.

                    MARTY
          Enough. Okay? <u>Everybody</u>.
               (to Michael)
          He's an asshole. But he knows it.
               (to Barry)
          And you're on the record. Okay?
               (to both)
          Everybody happy?

Nobody's happy. And here's JEAN with a nudge --

                    JEAN
          Don Jeffries is in the conference
          room...

                    MARTY
          Okay, we're coming...
               (to Barry)
          Tell them to bring the paperwork
          down when they're ready.
               (to Michael)
          Call Bob Nast, just see if they need
          help with this thing...
               (starting to walk away,
                then he stops, turns
                back--)
          You're welcome.

MICHAEL standing there, with THE ENVELOPE in one hand and
THE RED BOOKLET in the other. Standing there watching MARTY
and BARRY hustle away. All the power, all the oxygen,
leaving with them. The moment passing, as --

INT. LAW FIRM ELEVATOR -- DAY

Minutes later. Crowded. MICHAEL, looking shaky, fleeing
the office. And the door opens and --

INT. BUILDING LOBBY -- DAY (CONT)

MICHAEL stepping off the elevator. KAREN only a few feet
away. She's waiting to step onto another elevator car that's
also arrived. They pass within a yards of each other. Both
of them wrapped so tight just now they never even know it.

EXT. "TIM'S" -- NIGHT

Dark and forlorn. As we hear --

                    VERNE (OVER)
          Mercedes puts this little tag...

                    IKER (OVER)
          ...yeah, they shield that cable...

INT. THE TAURUS -- NIGHT (CONT)

Parked down the block. IKER on the driver's side. VERNE
beside him, holding a schematic drawing. Several bags and
boxes in the back and --

                    VERNE
          ...there's room here for the kel...
               (the schematic)
          ...once you tap into his GPS just make
          sure it's flush, we're packing
          the charge in the backseat armrest.

                    IKER
          Can I see it?
               (Verne opens the box,
                very carefully--)
          Could you make it any uglier?

                    VERNE
          It's a work of art.

                    IKER
          Who makes this?

                    VERNE
          Russian mafia. Albanians trying to
          look like Russian mafia. It's as far
          from the other thing as we can get.

IKER nods. VERNE carefully taking the box back.

INT. "TIM'S" BAR/DINING ROOM -- NIGHT

MICHAEL sitting on the bar watching ZABEL open a bank
envelope. Just the two of them.

                         ZABEL
          You said twelve...
                 (check in hand)
          This is seventy-five.

                         MICHAEL
          Don't get too excited.
                 (a bottle of vodka)
          You want a drink?

                         ZABEL
          I'm working.
                 (watching Michael serve
                  himself)
          So we're square then. No bad blood.

                         MICHAEL
          Just doing your job, right?

                         ZABEL
          That's it.

                         MICHAEL
          Everybody's got a job to do.

                         ZABEL
          Like it or not, right?

                         MICHAEL
          Like it or not.

ZABEL walks. MICHAEL alone in the dark, dead bar.

INT.   CHINATOWN CARD ROOM -- NIGHT

A basement hideaway on a slow night. We're back where we
started. MICHAEL at the table with THE PLUMBER, THE DEALER
and THE TWO OTHER PLAYERS.

                         MICHAEL
          Check.

                         PLAYER #2
          I go like that. Check.

THE PLUMBER starting to peel bills off his flashroll, as --

EXT. DOYERS ST. -- NIGHT

Chinatown late. Cold. Quiet. IKER walking up to THE
MERCEDES. He's holding a remote unit. Pressing it once.
Nothing. Again. Nothing. Third time's the charm. Lights
flashing as the alarm disables and --

INT. LAW FIRM LADIES ROOM TOILET STALL -- NIGHT

KAREN CROWDER -- <u>exactly where we first met her</u> -- sitting
fully dressed on the john. Hiding here. Trying to fight
off a panic attack using a breathing exercise she read about
in an airline magazine. Losing the battle, as --

INT. CHINATOWN CARD ROOM -- NIGHT

MICHAEL posts his blind --

                    PLUMBER
          So your bar, what happened? Just had
          to be in show biz, right?

INT. THE TAURUS -- NIGHT

Parked just down the block from the card room. VERNE at
the wheel. Eyes scanning. Operational energy.

INT. THE MERCEDES -- NIGHT (CONT)

IKER hard at it -- something not fitting under the dashboard
-- he's struggling -- sweating -- <u>bingo</u> -- he's got it --

INT. CHINATOWN CARD ROOM -- NIGHT

MICHAEL away from the table now, over by the metal detector.
He's just pulled his pager out of the shitty plastic basket,
trying to read the message and --

                    PLUMBER
                 (from the table)
          What're you doing? You just got here.

MICHAEL starts putting stuff into his pockets and --

                    PLUMBER
          Guy plays nine hands and walks away?
          What'd I do? I scare you away?

INT. THE MERCEDES -- NIGHT

IKER into the backseat now -- cutting open the armrest --

INT. CHINATOWN FREIGHT ELEVATOR -- NIGHT

Ascending. MICHAEL leaving in a hurry. Strapping on his
Rolex, trying to read the pager and --

INT.   THE MERCEDES -- NIGHT

IKER -- he's a machine -- pulling the bomb from a bag --
one hand wedging open the hole he's cut in the armrest --
trying to get the thing in there and --

INT.   CHINATOWN CARD ROOM HALLWAY -- NIGHT

A DOORMAN waiting as MICHAEL steps off the elevator and --

INT.   THE TAURUS -- NIGHT

VERNE -- seeing MICHAEL -- grabbing the radio --

                    VERNE
          -- abort! -- abort! -- he's out --
          he's on route -- abort! --

INT.   THE MERCEDES -- NIGHT

IKER -- not quite done -- fuck -- slapping the armrest back
into place and --

EXT.   PELL ST./CHINATOWN -- NIGHT

MICHAEL on the street -- on the phone -- heading up the block
toward Doyers Street and the Mercedes --

                    MICHAEL
               (walk and talk)
          Walter?

                    WALTER (PHONE/OVER)
          "Michael -- thank God, there you are.
          I have a problem -- big problem --"

INT.   THE MERCEDES -- NIGHT

IKER -- closing up shop -- grabbing his supplies -- fast --

                    VERNE (RADIO/OVER)
          "-- get out of there! --"

EXT.   PELL ST./CHINATOWN -- NIGHT

MICHAEL still on the phone -- on the way --

                    MICHAEL
          -- just now?

                    WALTER (PHONE/OVER)
          "-- I don't know -- ten, fifteen
          minutes ago -- he was driving home --"

EXT. DOYERS ST. -- NIGHT

IKER out of THE MERCEDES -- closing the door -- hitting his remote unit -- lights flashing as the alarm goes <u>on</u> and --

EXT. CORNER OF PELL AND DOYERS -- NIGHT

MICHAEL just turning onto Doyers Street -- pulling his remote security pendant and --

>   WALTER (PHONE/OVER)
>   "-- he didn't kill him -- he saw him
>   get up -- *try to get up* --"

UP THE STREET -- THE MERCEDES -- lights flashing as the alarm disables and --

>   MICHAEL
>   -- is he drunk?

>   WALTER
>   "--no that's the first thing I asked
>   him -- no, he's sober-- "

INT. THE TAURUS -- NIGHT

VERNE firing up the engine and --

EXT. CHINATOWN -- NIGHT

IKER walking away toward Canal Street and --

INT. THE MERCEDES -- NIGHT

MICHAEL jamming the car into gear -- peeling out into the street and --

EXT. CHINATOWN -- NIGHT

IKER turning as THE MERCEDES goes flying past -- <u>just</u> making the light -- squirting out onto Canal Street and --

INT. THE TAURUS -- NIGHT

VERNE skidding THE TAURUS to a stop -- door flying open -- IKER jumping in beside him -- and they're off again --

>   VERNE
>   -- are we good? --

>   IKER
>   -- it's in -- I don't know -- I had
>   no time -- I couldn't check it --

                         VERNE
               -- where the hell's he going? -- get
               that laptop up -- find him --

EXT. WEST SIDE HIGHWAY -- NIGHT

THE MERCEDES speeding North --

INT. THE MERCEDES -- NIGHT

MICHAEL trying to drive and mess with the GPS UNIT on his
dashboard. Something's wrong with it. He's tapping on it
and THE SCREEN is flickering on and off... Fuck it. He
slaps the GPS away -- steps on the gas and --

EXT. THE WEST SIDE HIGHWAY -- NIGHT

THE TAURUS in pursuit --

INT. THE TAURUS -- NIGHT

VERNE driving. IKER working A LAPTOP COMPUTER --

                         IKER
                 (tapping on the keyboard)
               -- it's his GPS -- it's in and out --
               he's up there somewhere --

                         VERNE
               Good news is he's heading out of town.

EXT. WEST SIDE HIGHWAY -- NIGHT

THE MERCEDES racing North toward the bridge, as we --

DISSOLVE TO

EXT. WESTCHESTER MANSION DRIVEWAY -- NIGHT/PRE-DAWN

THE WESTCHESTER MANSION DRIVEWAY. Four hours later. Just
before dawn. MICHAEL leaning against the MERCEDES, munching
on the stale baguette that's been in his car since Saturday.
Looking over as --

JERRY DANTE comes walking out of the house.

                         JERRY
               He's changing his shirt...
                 (pulling a cigarette as
                 he wanders over--))
               I talked to my guy at the State Police
               barracks. Better we go over there and
               surrender and they can tell the town
                         (MORE)

                        JERRY   (cont'd)
              cops to kiss off.
                   (lighting up, as--)

EXT.   COUNTRY ROAD -- NIGHT/PRE-DAWN

THE TAURUS parked on the shoulder of that quiet two-lane
outside the mansion gates. The hood is up. VERNE standing
there pretending that something's wrong with the motor and --

INT.   THE TAURUS -- NIGHT/PRE-DAWN (CONT)

IKER staring at his laptop, when suddenly --

                        IKER
              We got power -- it's on! -- it just
              went on! --

VERNE slamming the hood shut -- rushing around --

                        VERNE
              Let's make sure he's alone.

EXT. MANSION DRIVEWAY/COUNTRY ROAD -- NIGHT/PRE-DAWN

THE MERCEDES speeding away from the house --

INT.   THE TAURUS -- NIGHT/PRE-DAWN

VERNE and IKER not ready -- THE MERCEDES tearing ass out into
the road -- speeding off in the *other* direction and --

                        VERNE
              Fuck!

                        IKER
              I couldn't see -- did you see? --

                        VERNE
              He went the wrong way!

                        IKER
              Go! -- go! --

EXT.   WESTCHESTER COUNTRY ROAD -- NIGHT/PRE-DAWN

THE MERCEDES racing along.

INT.   THE MERCEDES -- NIGHT/PRE-DAWN

MICHAEL escaping. Driving wild. And this time around we
know what's in his head. Definitely running from more than
Mr. Greer and Jerry Dante.

INT.   THE TAURUS -- NIGHT/PRE-DAWN

VERNE driving hard.   IKER directing off the laptop screen --

> IKER
> -- right -- he took a right! --

> VERNE
> -- which one -- there's --

> IKER
> -- now he's --

> VERNE
> -- which right? --

INT.   THE MERCEDES -- NIGHT/PRE-DAWN

MICHAEL -- turning again -- aimless -- windows open -- cold
air whipping through -- braking suddenly -- impulsive --
turning -- suddenly -- faster now and --

INT.   THE TAURUS -- NIGHT/PRE-DAWN

Mounting panic.   Military style.

> IKER
> -- I don't know -- it's a left --

> VERNE
> -- I don't have a left! --

> IKER
> -- turn -- turn -- turn around! --

VERNE slamming on the brakes and --

EXT.   COUNTRY ROAD/THE FIELD -- DAWN

THE MERCEDES skidding to a stop.

PULL BACK TO REVEAL

THE HUGE OPEN PASTURE. Surrounded by forest. The sun just
starting to rise. Cold mist hanging over the whole valley.
Nothing but gray and green. Stark. Perfect.

INT.   THE TAURUS -- DAWN

VERNE and IKER are lost. All systems failing.

> IKER
> (pointing at the screen)
> -- he's stopped --

                    VERNE
        -- <u>where</u>? --

                    IKER
        -- I don't know -- we're close --
        I've got signal, but --

                    VERNE
        -- let me see it --

EXT. THE FIELD -- DAWN

MICHAEL out of the car. Jumping the fence. Walking into the
field. Behind him, the Mercedes with the engine running.

THE THREE HORSES poised at the crest of the pasture. Hanging
in the fog like ghosts. Watching MICHAEL come toward them.

MICHAEL'S FACE as he walks. Everything that's happened writ
large in these eyes. Everything he's done wrong. All the
things he hasn't done. Wounded and weary and humbled by the
abundance of his inadequacies. It is to weep...

And finally he stops. Just standing there.

INT. THE TAURUS -- DAWN

Still stopped there where we left them. VERNE now with the
laptop -- IKER scanning out the window --

                    VERNE
        -- we're on the other side --

                    IKER
        -- we went past it --

                    VERNE
        -- it's just over this hill --

                    IKER
        -- but he's stopped --

                    VERNE
        -- gimme the box -- give it! --

EXT. THE FIELD -- DAWN

MICHAEL standing there. The horses. The fog. The woods.

THE MERCEDES EXPLODES!

THE HORSES already running before MICHAEL can turn back --
pieces of the car that have been blown into the sky still
raining down before he's fully grasped what's happening --

MICHAEL simply shocked. Senseless. Standing there frozen.
Stunned. The car -- his car -- is <u>gone</u> -- replaced by a
skeletal shell of fire -- smoke pluming -- little follow-up
explosions popping every couple seconds. MICHAEL looks
around. Looks back. He should be dead. He is not.

And now, as the reality of that sinks in, as the smell of
burning car finally reaches him, we can see the confusion
drain away. All that staggered chaos in Michael's eyes
suddenly replaced with steel. He should be dead. He is not.

And now he's walking. <u>Toward</u> the car.

Walking faster. Determined.

He starts running -- running toward the fire and --

EXT.   THE NEARBY ROAD -- DAWN

THE PARKED TAURUS. VERNE and IKER standing there --

EXT.   THEIR POV -- DAWN

CLOUD OF SMOKE rising over the hill just in front of them.
Thick black smoke wafting up above the fog, as --

EXT.   FIELD/ROAD/BURNING CAR -- DAY

MICHAEL coming toward the car. Glancing around to make sure
he's alone. Wiping away at the smoke to get close.
Recoiling as another little explosion fuels the flames and
<u>he's throwing things into the burning frame of the car!</u>

The Rolex. His cell phone. His belt. A ring. Throwing in
anything that might survive the fire and --

EXT.   THE NEARBY ROAD -- DAY

VERNE and IKER have seen enough.

                    VERNE
          Better check it out.

EXT.   FIELD/ROAD/WOODS -- DAY

MICHAEL done throwing shit into the car. One last look
around and now he's running. Up into the woods. Scrambling
up the mountain, toward the trestle, into the sun, as...

INT.   THE LAW FIRM CONFERENCE ROOM -- DAY

FORTY PEOPLE -- ATTORNEYS -- ASSISTANTS -- PARALEGALS --
ACCOUNTANTS -- KAREN -- MARTY -- DON JEFFRIES -- all sitting

absolutely <u>silent</u> amidst the debris of an eighteen hour work session. ALL EYES ON --

BARRY hunched over a phone. Listening and listening and...

>   BARRY
>   (finally)
>   I'll tell him....of course...you
>   too...I'll check back.

And now he's hanging up the phone. Turning to the room.

>   BARRY
>   We have a deal.

A beat. And then someone starts to clap. And someone else.
And then they're all APPLAUDING -- MARTY -- DON JEFFRIES --
BARRY -- happy warriors all -- and as the backslapping and
smiles keep building.

THE CAMERA FINDS

KAREN hesitating. But only a moment. Because it's easier
then to join the party than not. Smiling now. Her tight
smile. But is she letting it in, or forcing it out?

EXT. WESTCHESTER STRIP MALL PARKING LOT -- DAY

A beat-to-shit Chevy Caprice rumbles into the lot. Stops
there. MICHAEL walking from a pay phone. He's wearing new
sneakers, new parka, knit hat pulled low. Getting in and --

INT. THE CAPRICE -- DAY (CONT)

TIMMY behind the wheel. Quiet. Tentative.

>   MICHAEL
>   (looking over)
>   <u>What</u>?

>   TIMMY
>   Thanks, Mick.

>   MICHAEL
>   Just get me out of here.

TIMMY nods. DROPS the car in gear, and --

INT. LAW FIRM MINI-CONFERENCE ROOM -- DAY

Glass box. BRINI, JEFF GAFFNEY, and TWO ASSOCIATES in the
middle of a meeting. Looking over as --

      PARTNER
    (at the door)
 Did you hear?

      GAFFNEY
 Yeah, they closed U/North.

      PARTNER
 No, about Michael Clayton...

      GAFFNEY
 What?

      PARTNER
 Car bomb. Upstate. This morning.
 He was killed.

      GAFFNEY
 What?

Someone in the hallway, calling THE PARTNER away from the
door and GAFFNEY rushing out to join the conversation and --

      FIRST ASSOCIATE
 Holy shit...

     SECOND ASSOCIATE
 Who's Michael Clayton?
   (turning to--)

BRINI. But she won't answer. Imploding. Holding herself.
Hand to her mouth. Pressing back against the tears that are
coming no matter what she does, as we --

INT. NEW YORK HOTEL BATHROOM -- DAY

KAREN at the mirror. Still wet from the shower --

      KAREN
 ...there had been a series of overtures
 from the plaintiffs dating back...
   (trying it again)
 Over the past several months we'd
 gotten word that the plaintiffs were
 considering settlement numbers...

INT. NEW YORK HOTEL GRAND BALLROOM -- DAY

A rushed meeting. THIRTY PEOPLE -- U/NORTH BOARDMEMBERS
and PRIMARY STOCKHOLDERS -- seated in a room that could hold
three hundred. Everyone has an information packet and a copy
of the lawsuit deal memo. SECURITY GUARDS manning the door.
And up front, addressing the assembled --

                    KAREN
             (smiling and confident)
        -- we'd also discovered that their
        legal fees were capped at thirty-two
        percent of the judgement up to four
        hundred million, and dropped to twenty-
        four percent after that, so we knew
        there was this motivational dead zone
        in the middle for them...

INT. NEW YORK HOTEL BEDROOM -- DAY

KAREN trying to choose a suit --

                    KAREN
        ...it was also at this time that...
            (reset)
        We had a meeting in June with the
        finance team and...
            (try again)
        We were informed by our finance team,
        last June that they'd run the numbers
        and that the benefits...

INT. NEW YORK HOTEL GRAND BALLROOM -- DAY

They're eating out of her hand.

                    KAREN
        ...that the tax benefit -- if we could
        keep the settlement under six-hundred
        million and get it done this fiscal
        year -- that the write-off would
        essentially pay for itself.

INT. NEW YORK HOTEL BATHROOM -- DAY

KAREN at the mirror putting on makeup.

                    KAREN
        We've negotiated..._requested_...we...
            (catching her reflection
             and almost losing it for
             a moment--)

INT. NEW YORK HOTEL GRAND BALLROOM -- DAY

THE BALLROOM. She's rolling now --

                    KAREN
        We have _insisted_ that Kenner, Bach &
        Ledeen cap it's fee at fifty million
        and we anticipate no further legal fees
        in the closing of this settlement.
                  (MORE)

                    KAREN (cont'd)
              (pausing for triumph)
         The package you have before you
         represents, in my judgement, the very
         strongest possible position for our
         company under the circumstances. As
         Chief Counsel it is my recommendation
         that the proposal be confirmed.

And she's done. And it's gone very, very well. Many happy
prosperous faces.

                    DON JEFFRIES
         Thank you, Karen.
              (taking over now)
         If you could just give us a few minutes
         to talk it over...

                    KAREN
              (with a smile))
         I'll be right outside.

EXT.   HOTEL BALLROOM FOYER -- DAY

The big, weird hub of three different huge reception rooms.
Wall-to-wall carpet. Chairs stacked in distant corners.
Empty. KAREN walking off her excitement. Standing there.

Catching her reflection in a wall of mirrors.

And then...

                    MICHAEL (OS)
         How'd it go?

She turns. Stops. Blinks. Freezes.

                    MICHAEL
         Pretty freaky, huh?
              (he's coming toward her)
         You see Arthur? He's hanging around
         here somewhere...

She's just paralyzed. He's carrying one of those copy-shop
boxes.

                    MICHAEL
         Hey, I'm kidding...
              (he smiles)
         C'mon. Lighten up.

He drops the box. Pulls out a RED-COVERED BOOKLET.

                    MICHAEL
You have one of these?
        (offering it)
Great memo. An oldie but a goodie.
        (she doesn't move)
Got your heart racing, don't I?

                    KAREN
I don't know what you think you're
doing...

                    MICHAEL
What do you think I'm doing?

                    KAREN
The suit is over. We have a deal.
This...
        (the memo)
Whatever this is, it's meaningless at
this point.

                    MICHAEL
You think?
        (so enjoying this)
I must've gotten it wrong. I heard
you had a tentative proposal. I didn't
realize you'd written all those checks
already. What a drag...
        (the box)
I've got thousands of these things,
what the hell am I gonna do?

                    KAREN
I'm calling Marty...

                    MICHAEL
Do it. Call him. That's a great place
to start. Let's find out who told him
Arthur was calling Anna Kysersun.
Let's find out who tapped those phones.

                    KAREN
...this...this memorandum...even if it
were authentic -- which I doubt -- I
highly doubt...

                    MICHAEL
I know what you did to Arthur.

                    KAREN
...even if it was, it would belong to
U/North, it would be protected...

MICHAEL
I know you killed him.

KAREN
...this is a cut-and-dried case of
attorney-client privilege!

MICHAEL
See that's just...
        (here comes the steam)
That's just not the way to go here,
Karen. For such a smart person, you're
lost, aren't you? You've got the
moves, but you don't hear the music.

KAREN
        (backing away)
...this conversation...this is over.

MICHAEL
I'm not a guy you kill! I'm the guy
you buy!
        (that stops her cold)
Are you so fucking blind you don't see
what I am? I'm the easiest part of
your whole problem and you're gonna
<u>kill</u> me? Don't you know who I am?
I'm a fixer! I'm a bagman! I do
everything from shoplifting wives to
bent congressmen and you're gonna blow
me up? What do you need, Karen? Lay
it on me. You want a carry permit?
Need a heads-up on an insider trading
subpoena? Need someone's name erased
from an escort service list? Got a
rich kid busted for dope? Somebody
beat up their mistress?
        (wide open)
I sold out Arthur for eighty grand
and a three-year contract and you're
gonna <u>kill</u> me?

KAREN
        (barely)
What do you want?

MICHAEL
What do I want? I want more. I want
out! And now, with this......
        (the memo)
I want everything.

KAREN
Is there a number?

                         MICHAEL
          Ten is the number.

                         KAREN
          Ten what? Ten million?
               (incredulous)
          Where do you think I can get ten
          million dollars?

                         MICHAEL
          You know what's so great about this?
               (the memo)
          Did you read to the end? You see who
          signed it? Let's go in that ballroom
          and ask Don Jeffries if he wants to
          pass the hat for a worthy cause.

     KAREN is reeling. She can hardly breathe.

                         KAREN
          This...it would have to be a longer
          conversation...and someplace else...

                         MICHAEL
          Where? My car?
               (on her hard now)
          Let's make it easy. Let's call it five
          to forget about Arthur's murder.

                         KAREN
          Five is easier.
               (hopeful for a moment)
          That would be something that we might
          be able to do. Five could work.

                         MICHAEL
          Great. And the other five million is
          to forget about the four-hundred-and-
          sixty-eight people who got wiped out by
          your weedkiller.

                         KAREN
          Let me finish this meeting. Let me
          talk to Don. Let me...

                         MICHAEL
          Do I look like I'm negotiating?

     Across the room -- THE DOOR TO THE BALLROOM OPENS and --

                         DON JEFFRIES
               (all smiles)
          Karen...

                    KAREN
               (over her shoulder)
          One second.

                    DON JEFFRIES
               (stepping out)
          ...everything okay?

                    KAREN
               (to Michael)
          Yes.

                    MICHAEL
          Ten million. Off shore. Bank of my
          choosing. Immediately.

                    KAREN
          Yes.

                    MICHAEL
          Say it.

                    KAREN
          Ten million dollars. Your bank.
          As soon as this meeting is over.

          MICHAEL hesitates. She's serious. It's his. Ten million.

                    DON JEFFRIES
               (insistent now)
          Karen, everyone's waiting...

                    KAREN
          I'm coming!
               (back to Michael--)
          So you...I'll just...we...

                    MICHAEL
          You're so fucked.

                    KAREN
          Excuse me?

                    MICHAEL
          You're fucked. It's over.
               (his pocket, his phone,
                flipped open, like it's
                on--)

                    KAREN
          What do you mean?

                    MICHAEL
          Take a wild guess.

                    DON JEFFRIES
               (coming toward them)
          Is there a problem?

                    KAREN
          I don't understand...

                    MICHAEL
               (the phone)
          Want me to take a picture while I'm
          at it?

                    KAREN
               (small and faraway)
          You don't want the money...?

                    MICHAEL
          Keep it. You're gonna need it.

                    DON JEFFRIES
          Is this fellow bothering you?

                    MICHAEL
               (to Karen)
          I think I'll let you tell him.

She can't make sense -- swamped -- lost --

                    DON JEFFRIES
          Karen, I've got the whole board sitting
          in there. What the hell is going on?
               (wheeling on Michael)
          Who are you?

                    MICHAEL
          I'm Shiva the God of Death.

MICHAEL starting to walk away and --

                    DON JEFFRIES
          Ron! Ronny!
               (yelling back toward the
                ballroom--)
          I need security out here immediately.
               (turning because--)

DALBERTO and TWO OTHER DETECTIVES are coming quickly from one
of the distant empty ballrooms and --

                    DON JEFFRIES
          Here we go...
               (thinking they're part of
                his team--)
          That guy, right there -- stop him --
                    (MORE)

> DON JEFFRIES (cont'd)
> grab that guy!
>> (but they don't)
> What're you doing?
>> (totally confused now
>> because--)

TWO SECURITY GUARDS are jogging out of the ballroom and --

> DALBERTO
> Slow down, guys...
>> (flashing his badge)
> Police Department. N.Y.P.D.

> DON JEFFRIES
> <u>What</u>?

KAREN just drifting to the floor and --

MICHAEL walking away. Leaving chaos in his wake.

There's DON JEFFRIES still carrying on and DALBERTO trying
to calm him down.

U/NORTH BOARDMEMBERS spilling out of the ballroom to see
what's going on.

KAREN sitting there on the floor in shock like some sort of
accident victim.

FINALLY

GENE waiting by the exit. Watching MICHAEL come toward him.
Headphones around his neck make it clear he's been listening
to the whole thing.

> GENE
> You okay?

They trade a look. MICHAEL has just torn off his skin.
Naked to the world.

> MICHAEL
> I need some air.

> GENE
> Sure, just...stay close.

MICHAEL nods. Walking away, as we --

<u>EXT. SIXTH AVENUE -- DAY</u>

Rush hour. MICHAEL walking -- walking toward the park --
walking through the sea of people and faces, as we begin to
hear the crazed, manic voice of --

                    ARTHUR EDENS (V.O.)
Michael. Look at me, Michael. Look at
me and make believe. Make believe it's
not just madness. Because it's not
<u>just</u> madness...

TAIL CREDITS begin --

                    ARTHUR EDENS (V.O.)
...I mean, <u>yes</u> -- okay, <u>yes</u> --
<u>elements</u> of madness -- the speed of
madness -- yes, the occasional,
euphoric, pseudo-hallucinatory moments
that, <u>yes</u> -- fine -- <u>agreed</u> --
distracting -- nostalgic -- all of
that -- but that's just the package
-- the plate -- think of it as a tax --
The Mania Tax -- The Insanity Tax --
or like advertising on TV -- it's the
freight -- the weight -- it's the price
of the show...

As we fade out and...

                    <u>**THE END**</u>

Q & A

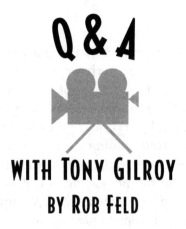

WITH TONY GILROY
BY ROB FELD

If we can start with a little background, your father, Frank Gilroy, is a play-wright and filmmaker. That must have impacted you somehow?

Tony Gilroy: In many ways. Just naturally you pick up the rhythms and atmosphere of what's going on around you. I remember as a child answering the phone when they called in the grosses from the theatre. So, it goes all the way back to that. There were always projects. There were always stories around, storytelling. But we didn't grow up in Hollywood. We grew up in upstate New York, a very conscious decision by my father to keep us away from all that. My father worked at home, so I never knew anything but a writer's life. When he was doing a film, he'd be gone for a couple of months, and then he'd be back home working in his pajamas. He worked early, he'd change at two o'clock, and his day was done and he was looking for someone to talk to.

So by osmosis I think, just from life, from dinner table conversation and everything, that's what you see, it's what you learn. It was a house full of books and I was a big reader early. I went to a school that was basically useless. I had a limited education, really, left at sixteen and was pretty much autodidactic about everything. I'd always been the type that, if I wanted to learn about something, I'd make a project out of it.

Rob Feld interviewed Tony Gilroy in New York City on August 8, 2007. Feld is a writer and independent producer at Manifesto Films. His writings on film and interviews with such noted filmmakers as James L. Brooks, Charlie Kaufman, Bill Condon, Peter Hedges, Noah Baumbach, Mike Nichols, and Alexander Payne appear regularly in *Written By* magazine and *DGA Quarterly*, as well as in the Newmarket Shooting Script® series.

Growing up, I had no intention of being a writer. I left home to be a musician and did that for ten or twelve years. I moved to Boston when I was sixteen and played up there for about six years, then started writing songs and seeing a couple hundred movies every year. I moved to New York City. I was changing, I guess, starting to write short stories and then working on a novel. I started sending stories out to serious magazines. It was the era of Raymond Carver—the rise of really hard, terse short fiction, which was a good thing to mimic starting out. And then I thought I'd get over it and get rich and write a screenplay, and it took me five or six years to figure out how to do it. I stopped playing music and started tending bar. I became a freak for writing screenplays—stopped writing stories, stopped writing fiction—I just became a student of that. That's all I did, with the hopes of getting paid for it.

Did you then sell a spec?

TG: No, I'd written a bunch of specs and nothing clicked. The very first one, people said, "Well, this kind of sucks, but there's something in here. Maybe you should do another one?" So I did, and then my brother Danny and I wrote together. We were a team for a while and that was great. I met Peter Cohn, who was working as a reader at New Line, when New Line was five desks down by the Port Authority. He read a script of mine and said, "They're not going to buy this, but do you want to write something with me?" He had this connection at Cannon Films and an idea, so we wrote a script—an original called *Cupid O'Malley Is as Dead as They Get*, for Chuck Norris. That was my first paying job and I quit tending bar—just in the nick of time, as my son was being born. It was an action mystery. Very 80s. Cupid O'Malley had this high-tech, Teflon, machine-gun kind of crossbow. He was a Vietnam vet, private eye in Southern California. We had the whole thing set against the backdrop of the South Vietnamese exile community in Garden Grove, California. Teflon crossbows and stolen semiconductor chips. But it never got made.

Did you get an agent from that?

TG: I had some phone numbers at ICM but I didn't actually have an agent. My brother Danny and I had written a script that people really loved called *Big Moose*. I'd also done a spec on my own called *R.S.V.P.*, a romantic comedy about a couple who invites the President to their wedding. They decide to break up but they're forced to stay together; another very 80s, sort of Preston Sturges comedy. That also didn't sell but it got me a job, and ICM took me on. I was working hard. I was a grinder. I kept at it and was good about not sitting on scripts. I was good about moving on and coming up with ideas, which turned out to be a key thing.

How do you think of a screenplay as a document in and of itself? It can be a rigid format but in your writing of them you find ways to break out of that, to get the reader to see the movie.

TG: The primary thing is to make the reading experience as identical to seeing the movie as possible. What I want is somebody to be able to read the movie in one hour and fifty-eight minutes. And I want the prose to match the tone of the movie. I want it to smell as much like the movie as it possibly can, so that when you're done reading the script you can say, *Wow, I just saw that and I know the person writing it saw it, too.* I don't ever want to be in the reader's way.

It's very difficult to be transparent and simple, but that's what I'm going for—and I'll change the voice of the script to do it. There are scripts I'll approach or format differently than others for that reason. I'll even lay out the pages in a certain way. For me, they turn into very cultish documents. I'm very obsessive. The final first draft versions of my scripts have been worked over in ways that have nothing to do with the movie or anything else. A lot of it's just compulsive.

I've written a couple of things since I directed, and I finished something for myself, and I'd thought, *Well, now that you're writing for yourself to direct, you won't have to do all of this stuff. You won't be as crazy and overwork the sentences and descriptions, and you won't be such a nut.* But, either I've done it too long to change, or maybe it's become a means of staying inside the material—staying interested—long enough to work it all out.

There was a software program that I used for many years, WordPerfect, which is what I learned on and what I loved, but it didn't paginate for you. So you had to pay attention to what was falling where, and it was very important to me never to have speeches break on pages. I would obsess, *God, I need to get rid of one line to make this fit.* And no matter how many times I'd pass through the script, I would *always* be able to find something to get rid of on any individual page. The fact that there was always something to get rid of on every page was a lesson. Every now and then I'd come to a page and go, *There isn't one thing that I can get rid of to buy a line, it's so strong.* I'll stare at a page for fifteen minutes, *Can I get rid of this? Can I get rid of that?* I've been doing that for twenty-five years.

But it's telling if you find you can always cut something, right?

TG: You end up with things that are propulsive. You end up with scenes that don't sit around. Come in late, get out early. When you finally start to get stuff made, the lesson's reaffirmed when you're sitting in dailies, watching your dialogue over and over and saying, *Oh, God, I didn't have to write that.* You learn how little you need. You start writing less and thinking more. You become very unforgiving about stuff. You get merciless.

*You mentioned individual script rules you make for yourself per project. What were your guidelines writing **Michael Clayton**?*

TG: I don't think there's any place in this script where I get very conversational with the reader. I wanted to reflect a pretty somber, rugged, simple tone, kind of flinty in its description. It needed a high degree of accuracy. If you're writing a movie where the behavior presents in a much more primary way, you don't have to articulate as much and you have more leeway. You don't have to be as careful, sometimes. If someone's yelling, "Hey, close down the perimeter," there isn't too much else to say. There's a lot of behavior in *Michael Clayton* that's finely calibrated, and you have to be very delicate with that. I wanted to make sure that all those rhythms were present; that when I thought there was any chance that someone might misinterpret the subtext of behavior, it was clear. But you have to be very careful if you're touching at the subtext. If it's really something underneath, you want the reader to feel it that way. You have to give them the smell of what it's like without overdoing. So I was very, very careful in many ways, I think, with this one.

You have these great parenthetical indicators, like Karen "having a lonely egg." That can give subtle hints.

TG: I'll tell you who I got that from. Very early on, I worked on a television show that Jay Presson Allen did, who was a great writer. I remember reading her scripts and she had the best stage directions. I didn't even realize stage directions could do that. They were there, they weren't in your way, and you were happy they were there and they were *rhythmic*. You can't be writing *pause* and *beat* all of the time. You want to, but if you're really seeing your movie and you really care, stage directions really give you an opportunity to make sure you're setting a drumbeat for the dialogue. And over the years, I've probably developed a whole stock company of phrases and hesitations that I can draw on, but it's best when you find one that's dead-on specific. There's a lot of work that goes into it. If I don't have one, I'll leave a place holder and come back and find it. There have been times when stage directions have changed ten times before they've gotten accurate.

Because you were directing Michael Clayton *yourself, were you trying to speak more to actors in the script than usual?*

TG: No, that's really dangerous. Actors don't like stage directions, by and large. One of the biggest compliments I ever got from an actor was, "The first thing I do is go through and cross out all of the stage directions. I started doing that with your script and I realized you weren't telling me what to do. You were just telling what was going on." So, you have to be very careful. I mean, did anybody write worse stage directions than Eugene O'Neill? They almost make the plays unreadable. You want to have actors be able to feel that the person who's writing this really knows what's going on; isn't getting in their way, is informing them, and isn't slowing them down.

Did you rehearse much with the actors?

TG: I didn't. I think rehearsals are often better for the writer than anybody else. But I almost lost my nerve as we got closer.

And started having rehearsals?

TG: You know, you're tempted. You want everything to be prepared as Day One gets closer, particularly if it's your first time out. If you're a writer, as well, you're used to being prepared and dug in, so the urge to organize and line everything up is powerful. Just at the end, when I got a little nervous, I talked to Sydney Pollack, who said, "I don't do it either. I hate rehearsals. You're doing the right thing." I cast *Michael Clayton* really diligently and I like the idea that everybody was showing up every day super-prepared. *They* were nervous. I talked to another director who said on one movie he only rehearsed half his actors because it was a split location. He said the half he rehearsed showed up and were all over the place, wanting to talk and keep the process going. The half that hadn't rehearsed showed up ready to work, on point, energized. I don't know if I would always do it this way, but it worked for this film.

You had a lot of directors on your producing team: Anthony Minghella, Sydney Pollack, Steven Soderbergh, George Clooney.

TG: Yeah, I know. Because there was no money involved I could keep accumulating people. I had Castle Rock, but they couldn't really make the movie. Then Sydney read it, came on, helped with the script a little and gave me momentum. Then Soderbergh, who I was working with, read it and called me back and said, "We've got to do this movie for, like, nothing and have George do it." So he sent it to George, who said, "Well, I'll do it, but I want to direct it. I don't want to meet this guy." That meeting would take another two years to put together. The reality is, if this had been a money-making proposition for anybody, it would have been impossible to keep accumulating all of these people, and it turned out to be incredibly fortu-itous—it took so long to put the picture together that it became like a tag team. I'd need someone to call this person or that actor who wasn't calling me back, and Sydney would be off, busy somewhere, but Steven would be free that month. Then *he'd* be gone but Sydney would be here, and I'd be call-ing him. Then, at the end, Castle Rock became hugely important because we went back to Warner Brothers for distribution, where they have great rela-tionships. So, if it was by design, I'd be a genius, but it was totally shambolic.

Was it a spec script when you wrote it?

TG: No, it was a job. I'd done several scripts for Castle Rock—*Dolores Claiborne, Extreme Measures,* and then *Proof of Life.* My stock was pretty high there and I pitched it in a two-minute meeting. I said, "Martin [Shafer], I want to write a film for me to direct based in New York, about a lawyer who's a fixer at a law firm. It'll be a movie-star part and it won't be that expensive. Somebody will die, but we'll never go near a courtroom." That was it and he bought it, but I just got totally hung up doing other things. This was just when the *Bourne* saga began, and I had no idea what that was going to become—it started as an outline and went on for eight years—and we were just starting to shoot *Proof of Life.* So *Michael Clayton* ended up getting hor-ribly delayed along the way.

Much of what you've written has to do with secrets and conspiracies, which are constants in so much of storytelling. I was wondering how you think about them or what role they play for you?

TG: I don't think in terms of secrets as much as conflict. I don't know how you tell a story when people are getting along. One of the really big ways for people *not* to get along is when someone's not telling the truth.

How do you think about the parceling out of information in a suspense story—giving the audience what they need at certain points or keeping from them what you don't yet want them to know? Is that totally instinctual?

TG: I have no method. I have no rule about what's supposed to happen when, but I do have a lot of techniques I use to make those kind of movies work.

Such as?

TG: I do a lot of role playing. There's just no substitute for me when I'm trying to plot something out. Particularly if it's a *who-knows-what?* type of film. I'm either doing it on paper—having a conversation with myself—or if I've got someone to work with, just playing it out. I just worked with a director who turned out to be an amazing story director, but had never beaten out a story before, and it was *that* kind of movie. First day in, trying to figure it out, I started talking it through: *Okay, I'm Jack and this is what I know. I get up and I go to the paper and I do this, and this comes on my desk, and this is what I know ..."* And after an hour of this he says, "Are we going to do this all the way through?" And I said, "We're going to do this for every-body all of the time." It's *What would I do? What would I do next?* When I was starting out, I never wanted to work like that because it's unpleasant and it really is hard. It's chalkboard-like work—it's behavioral math—but after a while the disagreeableness of it, the unpleasantness and the hard work of it, pales in comparison to the time you've wasted when you *don't* do it. It's like quitting smoking or something. The pain of the alternative is just too great. It's just like, *I've got to go do this*, and finally you become a mule in the plow and you do it. I always resist it, but there's no substitute. I've got to put myself there, be the character and get rigorously down inside of it. But in terms of information? What I'm going to let the audience know and when? I don't know. I don't have any rules. I want to have great scenes. I want you to want to know what happens next.

I think because I'm empathizing with the character, I always have this impression when watching a suspense movie that I don't know as much as I actually know; I feel like I haven't been told the things that I clearly have been, which have made me feel anxious for the character I'm following.

TG: If it's right, when it's really done well, you should have everything. When something's really on point, when it really makes sense and it really is what the person would do—when it's both inevitable and completely sur-prising, that's when you're in the sweet spot. That's what you have to constantly be going for. That's the gold standard for good, imaginative storytelling.

Did you outline **Clayton?**

TG: Man, I fucked it all up. *Clayton?* I really messed up. I'm a huge outliner. It's sort of evolved into this three- or four-stage process, and the out-line is the next-to-last thing that I do. I had gotten very organized over time about writing scripts, and I'd gotten good about a process that worked for me. I have an accumulation stage where I gather all kinds of materials, make a big compost heap of dialogue and scene ideas, and research moments and too many files and documents—basically this big out-of-control mess. While that's going on, I'm trying to find the movie for myself. Sometimes that answer comes very early on, but sometimes not. So, maybe I'm building that pile of materials while I'm trying to find the movie. Maybe I know where the movie is, but I'm still gathering ideas. But, I'd gotten very good at taking that mass of shit, putting on the brakes, and saying, *Okay, enough, I've had this in my head for three months and I know everything I need to know. Stop.* Then I try to write a very detailed, scene-by-scene block-out of the whole movie as quickly as possible—under the best circumstances, four days or a week—sketch out the whole movie, sloppy pages, sketch dialogue, whatever comes out.

Before *Michael Clayton* I'd written a script called *Wild Kingdom*, which was about paparazzi and celebrity. I'd done all the research and was just about to start that outlining process—I was champing at the bit to do it—when I went out to pick up the newspaper and Princess Di had been hounded into the wall in Paris, which was pretty much identical to a scene I was planning to set with one of my characters on the Pacific Coast Highway. And for the next six weeks on television, everybody was saying all of the brilliant, unique things that my script was hoping to say. I told Disney, "I'm not doing this anymore. I can't do it now. It's not fresh anymore." They thought it made it better and tried to convince me to do it, but I was lost. So, I boxed up all this intense work. Six months later, Susan Lyne came to me and said, "Look, we would still pay you to write this. You can do anything you want to do, change it in any way. Why don't you take one more look at it?" I knew I couldn't do the same movie I was gonna do before, so I went back in, opened the box, and started changing stuff. I guess it must be what it's like for a painter when you work over an existing canvas; I was rubbing out and pasting over, there was old stuff coming through, new stuff layered on top, and, as I worked, the script took on this whole tertiary feel to it. It was really free. I loved what came out of it. It really was the most exciting writing experience I'd ever had and I thought, *Oh, well now I know how I should be writing scripts. This is my "White Album." This is the next level. I've spent all those years getting systems formalized and now this is the breakthrough, free thing. From now on this is how I write scripts.*

So, when I finally got down to *Michael Clayton*, which is incredibly rich material, that was my plan. The law firm provided this great canvas, there were a million ways the character could go, I had the whole "Realm and Conquest" thing with the son—I don't want to tell you how many hundreds of pages of crap I have written about that—I had all these *things* and felt they were all happening and I should honor them all. So I'd work in this direction for a week, then go in that direction for a month. And then I couldn't even find all of the files, but I figured, *Well, not to worry because this is how you got there with* Wild Kingdom. But a point came where I was so lost, I was so out there, that I became afraid to go to work. It wasn't writer's block, it was different, I was literally *afraid* to go to work. Afraid to admit how lost I'd gotten. I'd worked myself into a very serious panic about it, but I finally forced myself to open all of these files—I don't even know how many dozens of files and hundreds of pages—and I thought, *You know what? You don't even know what the time frame of the movie is. You've been on this thing for eight months or whatever, and you don't even know if the movie takes place over three months or three . weeks. You don't know anything. You're an absolute* poseur, fauxhemian *and if you were watching yourself, you'd be abusive. If by the end of the week, you don't know what the time frame of the movie is, you're going to have to walk away. You've got to move on, take a job and get back to whatever it was you used to do before.* The next day I thought, *Oh, this movie can take place over four days,* and I wrote the script in no time. It was ridiculous. I was trying to graft a method from another project onto *Michael Clayton.* Maybe there's another script that wants to be written that way, but it was not this script.

So then you outlined?

TG: Yeah, at that point I was so panicked I got very organized. I had some navigational scenes along the way, which is a thing for me—to have some scenes that I can count on, that tell me what the movie is about. I've never worked on anything where I didn't get completely script-blind along the way, and that's why the outlines are so critical, why knowing what your movie is about is imperative. I don't care what it is, I won't take a job if I don't know what the movie is. If I can't say, *Oh, this is a movie about* this, or, *I know what kind of movie this is,* I won't go near it. But even knowing what the movie is and having an outline, it doesn't matter, you just get blind sometimes. You get to page 87 and you're going, *Oh, my God this so complicated, I can't keep all of this in my head, and I'm working eighteen hours a day and there's too much going on in here and I can't remember why I thought this was good...*Then you get to the end, you clear it all away, clean it all down and then get rid of all the crap, and suddenly it's simple. And then you go, *Oh, wow! It's that. That's all* *it is. Why didn't I just do that to begin with?* Because it's just so hard to be simple. An incredible amount of effort goes into it. I don't know. I think it's true for painters, composers, dancers. You're always fighting for simplicity. It's really hard to get there.

When did that decision come to go nonlinear, to start with the future and then jump back? Did you initially think of it that way, or was that a problem-solving technique?

TG: It was there before it was useful, probably because one of the anchor scenes for me, one of the scenes that I had early on and that was a real North Star for me, was the hit-and-run scene at the Greer Mansion, where Michael comes in. I had the energy of it, how it works, the wife, the whole thing.

That's the self-realization scene where he says, "I'm not a miracle worker, I'm a janitor."

TG: Right. I had that scene sketched and somehow, instinctively, I knew I wanted that early. But, I thought, *where does he go from there?* But the utility of not having it be linear became clear long after I had started down that path. I liked what it did to the script. I liked coming back to the field and the car exploding and restarting the story. I liked having the energy of suspense kick in late. But even that turned out not to be the best thing about it. As we got close to filming, the possibilities that this replayed scene offered became clear, and that's when something that you've done either by mistake or through good instincts comes around to be crucial. Because, yes, it's definitely an energy boost to the final twelve minutes of the film. *What is going to happen now?* But in a much deeper way, it turned out to be such a critical element in understanding Michael Clayton's character. Seeing him there in that field the second time, knowing now what's led him there, it's just huge to be able to be there again. To really witness it. You can actually be completely with him. In a non-cheesy way, it's almost like a visual voiceover. Everything about movies is manipulative, but in a more hidden way coming back for the second time, you have a chance to be there with George in this rock-bottom moment and know that you're there for a reason. So the short answer is it worked, but it was there before I was aware of the various ways that it would be helpful.

It's not just the same footage, right?

TG: There's one piece of coverage of George that's a little bit different, that goes a little deeper the second time. It was by choice, but we were also very restricted in the shooting. We could only shoot that sequence for six minutes in the morning and six minutes in the afternoon, because it's taking place at dawn, a very specific moment in time. So, we shot for five days, six minutes in the morning, six minutes in the evening. Months before, we went up to that field eight or nine times. Robert Elswit and I went up there and videotaped all of our coverage, took it to the cutting room and edited it. We even had the First AD, Steve Apicella, put a cardboard horse up on the hill. It was planned like a military operation. We ended up with very specific coverage we wanted to get.

You open the movie with a long soliloquy, like some Howard Beale monologue in **Network***, which is kind of ballsy. Did you initially conceive of it like that, and did you get any resistance to it?*

TG: Yes. It was there from the beginning. We never had a problem with it. There was no resistance when we were making the movie because we had no adult supervision whatsoever. Nobody was telling us what to do. So, we were free and clear and everybody was way into that speech. It's pared down in the film a little bit, but not much. What's interesting is when we went to the editing room, I hadn't yet shot the opening sequence. We'd left it for post. In the first draft of the script it was designed to be this dreamy helicopter shot up Sixth Avenue. I knew I was never going to get that shot and honestly, my taste about the movie had changed over the years I was trying to get it made. So I wasn't trying for that. I'd decided it was going to be a lot of shots around the law firm, establishing the place. What was fascinating were the limitations on the visual imagery that we could put against Arthur's speech. Whether it's the complexity, or the suddenness, or whatever, it was incredibly restrictive on competing information. For example, you cannot show a face against that voice-over. The moment a face appeared, you'd immediately rush to connect it to the voice. Then I had all these gorgeous shots—these law firms have all of these conveyor belts and machines—I'd go to these law firms at night, make all these little camera rigs, put cameras on carts and baskets and conveyor belts and send them riding around. I gathered all this very cool footage, but most of it was just too complex, too challenging. It made you carsick to listen to Tom's voice-over and watch it all. I spent two months while Johnny [Gilroy] was editing, with all my little digital cameras on little rigs and carts, taking them around the Brill building, making shots, trying to make mockups that I could put on the computer against the speech to see what might work. That's when I came up with this whole cart concept that starts the film. So, it ended up being a six-week education. I finally went back to the firms with another DP, Tony Wolberg. We went at night for a week with a reduced crew, and made these tableau shots that are now at the beginning of the film. It was a real science project. I learned an incredible amount.

How did you research or find that bipolar voice? Have you had experience with it before?

TG: I've encountered two people in my life in the midst of manic breakdowns. So, I've seen the spectacular side of it up close. Maybe I'm not completely exempt from some of the edges of that. There are times where you feel that everything is significant, and there are days where you don't. Somehow it wasn't hard to imagine all of that.

How do you think about opening moments in general? How to bring an audience into a movie, introduce them to a character?

TG: It's absolutely critical how you start a movie. It's also the stuff you stare at longest as you write. Nothing gets quite as worked over. But then every single moment counts. Every word all along the way is critical. Nothing is extra. If you sit down and flip through your script and there's a page that you just don't want to look at, it shouldn't be there. There's something wrong with it. You have to ask yourself why you don't want to look at page 43. Everything matters.

You give your audience a good deal of credit by not spoonfeeding them information. You never have some expository scene, for example, where somebody mentions Michael's ex-wife. He just goes and picks up a kid and we go, "Oh, I know what that is. I recognize that."

TG: You know what? I was able to do it because I was directing the movie and because the movie was going to cost under $20 million. But I try to do it all of the time. People know what real life looks like, you know? And if you can get away with it, there's lots of artful ways of passing along information. Sometimes you play it too close to the bone and people don't get it and you've got to explain. Sometimes it's perfect and the people you're working with are too thick to see it. I've been fighting that fight forever. Sometimes you win and sometimes you lose. If it's your show, you win.

Michael Clayton *is a character study, but is it structured like a suspense film, like a* **Bourne** *film? Is the essence of the genre the same or are they really two different animals?*

TG: I only know this: more than anything, I'm *desperate* to hold on to people's attention. There's a pathological fear that I have that I'm going to lose your attention. I think that whatever craven deficiency that is in me gives some kind of urgency to how I'm going to write, no matter what it's going to be. I want you to be involved in every page, needing to know what happens next.

But, I don't see *Michael Clayton* as a thriller and I'm surprised when I hear people describe it that way. To me it's about soul sickness, about *how* we're bent to the wheel, *how* the decisions are made, *how* these moral compromises happen. It's the awful combination of fear and self-preservation. It's inertia, and why and how people make terrible decisions or escape from them. You see Arthur coming off the wheel and Michael wrestling with it. You're watching Karen Crowder, who's completely unprepared for the decisions that she's about to make, become as much a victim as anybody. In this script I'm much more interested in that moment where people decide to drive past the exit; when they make that mistake. This is a hero who's really way past the redemption highway before he turns around. And with Arthur, it's great that he's on the road to Damascus now, but where's he been for six years? So, for me, it was much more about compromise and moral dilemma. The thriller's the movie tax, isn't it? And not in a bad way. That's the price of telling the story. Like I said to Castle Rock in the pitch, *someone will* die. It's dessert.

What films were you screening as you prepared to direct **Michael Clayton?**

TG: We were really digging back into all of the 1970s movies that I grew up with. Pakula, John Boorman, Hal Ashby, Mike Nichols, Sydney, too many to mention. Robert Elswit and I had an extended cinema party even before we started pre-production. We knew we wanted the look to be raw and cold. We shot anamorphic and used a lot of old lenses with some real history and quality to them. We evolved into a very formal, nonmoving camera idea; very much about the frame. A lot of empty space. People in exile. If you look at it, there's very little background in the movie. There's always a lot of negative space, a lot of single people in empty rooms, empty places. People alone. The most direct visual reference, I guess, would be *Klute*.

How did you think about the music for this film?

TG: It's funny, I was a musician for years but I never had a clue on this movie what to do with it. I figured I'd know what music to use, that I should have some idea of the vibe, but I never had a *clue*. I never listened to any music for it, we cut the film, we watched the film dry, and I actually liked it dry. It almost worked. Every time we tried to put music against it, it rejected it. We watched it for a month with nothing on it, and I can totally see the attraction. People thought I was nuts. It was a tough, tough decision, and James Newton Howard came at us really hard to do the score. James was kind of huge and it made me nervous—it was almost too good to be true. I was worried we'd be committing to some huge score, but it was the opposite. James turned out to be the perfect co-conspirator and got exactly what we were up against—just a fantastic, icing-on-the-cake post-production experience.

How do you think about the environments you create for your characters? You're very specific in the scripts, too, about their homes, offices...

TG: These are real places to me. A lot of this job is journalism. You're trying to accurately report on the movie you're imagining. The saddest thing is reading a script where you feel the writer hasn't seen the movie they're writing. I check out immediately if I don't think somebody's there. But what's more complicated is somebody who's really seeing the movie but isn't a good reporter. They can't express it.

It's another form of character description, too.

TG: Absolutely, absolutely. It's wardrobe, isn't it? You can get carried away; it has to read the way you see it. There's a limited amount of thoughts that the audience or the reader can take. You can overload them. Catching the environment on the page can't take any longer than it would take for them to look at it and go, *Oh, I know what this place is like. I've been in a place like that. There's paint chipping off the radiator or the felt on the pool table is ripped.* You try and find the one detail that catches it all. You can't take any longer than that.

There are scenes in the script that didn't make it into the film.

TG: There's two characters that are in the script that got left on the cutting-room floor. The first one is just after the Greer scene, where Michael's waiting outside and Jerry Dante comes out to give him the rundown. It's a tight scene and it was really well played—we shot it—but this was just something that came out for time. We just finally didn't think we absolutely needed to mark the moment. What I miss is the thing that Jerry Dante asks for at the end, the favor for his cousin. But so be it.

The bigger edit was Brini. You'll see in the script there's a scene where Michael arrives at work and rides up the elevator. It's a bullshit scene—and again, we shot all this—but the reason for it was to lay the groundwork for the later scene between Michael and Brini, where you realize that their relationship is a secret. The scene between them in Michael's apartment was terrific. Jennifer Ehle, who's just an amazing actor, was perfect. George was perfect. It was exactly what I wanted—just this brittle, deadly episode between two people who've been sleeping together without a reason for just a little too long. It was another dead-end for Michael. Another loss. This scene stayed in till the final cut. We were just a little long and at that last cull, where you're putting everything on the table. And honestly, there'd been some opinions along the way that maybe we should revive Brini—there were people who saw the scene in a way I'd never, ever intended, that it was a connection that Michael should somehow cling to—that maybe we should bring her back at the end. I so hated that idea, to me this was such an empty relationship, and I was so down on the idea that anyone might misinterpret and think that there was something good going on here—I came into the editing room and said, "Let's try without it." And it came out like nothing.

The big loss was the story George tells about Jeff Gaffney and his wife. That hurt. It's a big tell on who he is and how low he's gotta go to do his job. The big benefit was losing the elevator scene that I never much liked, and when it came to pulling Brini out of the apartment, it turned out that we had lucked into just the right coverage to make it possible. In like fifteen minutes it was out without an echo. There's still one shot of Jennifer Ehle in the conference room at the end when they come in to say *Michael's dead*. The hardest part was calling the two actors—who'd both been nothing but perfect—and breaking the news. But the scenes are here, maybe we'll put them on the DVD.

CAST AND CREW CREDITS

Warner Bros. PICTURES
In association with Samuels MEDIA and
Castle Rock ENTERTAINMENT
Present
a Mirage ENTERPRISES/Section EIGHT production

"MICHAEL CLAYTON"

written and directed by
Tony GILROY

produced by
Sydney POLLACK
Steven SAMUELS

produced by
Jennifer FOX
Kerry ORENT

executive producers
Steven SODERBERGH
George CLOONEY
James HOLT
Anthony MINGHELLA

director of photography
Robert ELSWIT A.S.C.

production designer
Kevin THOMPSON

edited by
John GILROY A.C.E.

music by
James Newton HOWARD

costume designer
Sarah EDWARDS

casting by
Ellen CHENOWETH

George CLOONEY   Tom WILKINSON   Tilda SWINTON   Sydney POLLACK
Michael O'KEEFE   Ken HOWARD   Denis O'HARE   Sean CULLEN   Merritt WEVER
David LANSBURY   David ZAYAS   Robert PRESCOTT   Terry SERPICO   Bill RAYMOND

CAST
(In order of appearance)

Arthur Edens	Tom Wilkinson
Barry Grissom	Michael O'Keefe
Marty Bach	Sydney Pollack
Voice of Bridget Klein	Danielle Skraastad
Karen Crowder	Tilda Swinton
Michael Clayton	George Clooney
Chinese Dealer	Wai Chan
Player #1	Alberto Vazquez
Player #2	Brian Koppelman
Voice of Walter	Tom McCarthy
Mr. Greer	Denis O'Hare
Mrs. Greer	Julie White
Henry Clayton	Austin Williams
Ivy	Jennifer Van Dyck
Gerald	Frank Wood
Auctioneer	Richard Hecht
Gabe Zabel	Bill Raymond
Voice of Del	Jonathan Walker
Pam	Sharon Washington
Voice of Wendy	Cynthia Mace
Voice of Evan	Michael Countryman
Don Jeffries	Ken Howard
Interviewer	Amy Hargreaves
Secretary	Susan Pellegrino
Maude	Rachel Black
Todd	Matthew Detmer
Jail Guard	John Douglas Thompson
Anna	Meritt Wever
Deposition Lawyer	Brian Poteat
Lieutenant Elston	Christopher Mann
Milwaukee Captain	Edward Furs
Third Year	Katherine Waterston
Correction Officer	John Gerard Franklin
Fifth Year	Remy Auberjonois
Fourth Year	Pun Bandhu
First Year	Jason Strong
Mr. Verne	Robert Prescott
Caddy	Paul Oquist
Mr. Iker	Terry Serpico
Anna's Sister	Heidi Armbruster
Cindy Bach	Pamela Gray
Voice of UNorth	Andrew Sherman
Raymond Clayton	Kevin Hagan
Stephanie Clayton	Julia Gibson
Gene Clayton	Sean Cullen
Michelle	Susan Egbert
Timmy Clayton	David Lansbury

Detective Dalberto . . . . . . David Zayas
Jeff Gaffney . . . . Doug McGrath
Cop . . . . Gregory Dann
Cop #2 . . . . Cathy Diane Tomlin
Copy Kid . . . . Sam Gilroy
Attorney #1 . . . . Maggie Siff
Barry's Assistant . . . . Sarah Nichols
Jean . . . . Susan McBrien
Partner . . . . Jordan Lage
First Associate . . . . Neal Huff
Second Associate . . . . Paul Juhn
Poker Consultant . . . . Mike Scelza
Stunt Coordinator . . . . Jery Hewitt
Stunts . . . . Chris Barnes
                Norman Douglass
                Gene Harrison
                Don Hewitt
                Joanne Lamstein
                John E. Mack

Unit Production Manager/Co-Producer
. . . . Christopher Goode
First Assistant Director . . . . Steve Apicella
Second Assistant Director . . . . Michael Pitt
Music Supervisor . . . . Brian Ross
Art Director . . . . Clay Brown
Art Department Coordinator
. . . . Alyson Wellins Lewin
Property Master . . . . Peter Gelfman
Assistant Property Master . . . . . Jim Kent
Assistant Props . . . . Robin Voth
Set Decorators . . George DeTitta, Jr, SDSA
                Charles M. Potter
                Paul Cheponis
                Christine Mayer
Leadperson . . . . Chris DeTitta
Foreman . . . . John Oates Jr.
On Set Dressers . . . . Tom Joliat
Set Dressers . . . . Paul Gaily
                Tim Power
                Pete Shevlin
                Joe DeStefano
Special Artwork By . . . . John Miserendino
Post Production Supervisor
. . . . Charlene Olson
"A" Camera Operator . . P. Scott Sakamoto
"A" Camera First Assistant . . . Barry Idoine
"A" Camera Second Assistant
. . . . Angela Bellisio

"B" Camera Operator . . . . . Joe Collins
"B" Camera First Assistant
. . . . Gregor Tavenner
"B" Camera Second Assistant
. . . . Beka Venezia
Playback Operator/Video Assist
. . . . T Ray Treece
Still Photographer . . . . Myles Aronowitz
Sound Mixer . . . . Michael Barosky
Boom Operator . . . . . Daniel Rosenblum
Cable . . . . Jerry Yuen
                Michelle Mader
Script Supervisor . . . . . . Mary Cybulski
Assistant Costume Designer
. . . . Wade Laboissonniere
Wardrobe Supervisors . . . David Davenport
                Kate Edwards
Set Costumer . . . . Fionnuala Lynch
Makeup Department Head
. . . . Chris Bingham
Key Makeup Artist . . . . Mia Thoen
Hairstylist Department Head
. . . . Waldo Sanchez
Key Hairstylist . . . . Jerry Popolis
Chief Lighting Technician . . Scott Ramsey
Assistant Chief Lighting Technician
. . . . Michael J. Maurer
Rigging Gaffer . . . . . . Rocco Palmieri
Key Grip . . . . Gary Martone
Dolly Grip . . . . Robert Feldmann
"B" Dolly Grip . . . . Edward J. Knott III
Best Boy Grip . . . . . . Pedro Hernandez
Key Rigging Grip . . . . . Robert Kummert
Best Boy Rigging Grip . . . Daniel Beaman

2nd Unit Photography

Director of Photography . . . . . Joe Collins
Additional Director of Photography
. . . . Steven Finestone
"A" Camera Operators . . . . . John Young
                Patrick Quinn
Chief Lighting Technician . . Steve Ramsey
Key Grip . . . . Robert Kummert

Additional Photography

Director of Photography
. . . . Anthony Wolberg
1st Assistant Camera . . . . . Douglas Foote
2nd Assistant Camera . . . . Thomas Cioccio
Set Decorator . . . . John Schabel
Chief Lighting Technician . . Jon Montgomery
Key Grip . . . . John Duvall
Grip . . . . James Brown
U North Commercial . . . . Fluid

Visual Effects by . . . . . Handmade Digital Asylum
Location Manager . . . . Eddy Collyns
Assistant Location Managers . . Hilary Smith
David Ginsberg
Construction Coordinator
. . . . Michael Herlihy
Construction Foreman . . Michael Curry Jr.
Transportation Captain . . Dennis Salomone
Transportation Co-Captain
. . . . Kevin R. Wood
Parking Coordinator . . . . Jose Tejada
Parking Assistant . . . . Juan E. De La Rosa
Production Accountant . . . . J.R. Craigmile
Production Controller
. . . . Catherine Lynch Sullivan
First Assistant Accountant . . . . Abby Bailey
Assistant Unit Production Manager
. . . . Alyson Evans
Second Second Assistant Directors
. . . . Matt Power
Jason Ivey
Production Supervisor . . . Igor Srubshchik
Production Coordinator . . . . Jen Crammer
Assistant Production Coordinator
. . . . Amy Trachtman
Production Secretary . . . Joshua Chaplinsky
Production Staff Assistants. . Jessalyn Haefele
Adam Freelander
Samuels Media Production Supervisors
. . . . Roger DaPrato
Milan Popelka
Lauren Flaster
Assistant to Tony Gilroy
. . . . Niki DiCesare
Assistant to Jennifer Fox . . Dylan Ashbrook
Assistant to Kerry Orent . . . . Karla Nappi
Assistants to Steven Samuels . . Karen Marsh
Ann Marie Doris
Assistant to George Clooney
. . . . Angel McConnell
Security for Mr. Clooney
. . . . Giovanni Zeqireya
Casting Associate . . . . Amelia Rasche
Set Staff Assistants . . . . . . Megan Asbee,
Hilary Benas, Kit Bland, Kim Dellechiaie,
Melissa Mugavero, Paul Polow,
Chris Ryan, Loren Sklar,
Graham Smith, Justin Trimm
First Assistant Editor . . . . . Aaron Marshall
Second Assistant Editor . . . Ulysses Guidotti
Supervising Sound Editor . . . . Paul Soucek
Re-recording Mixers . . . . . Michael Barry
Andrew Kris

Dialogue Editor . . . . Dan Korintus
ADR Editor . . . . Kenton Jakub
Sound Effects Editor . . . . Brian Langman
Foley Editor . . . . . William Sweeney III
First Assistant Sound Editor . . . Daniel Ward
Foley Artist . . . . Jay Peck
ADR Mixer . . . . David Boulton
Bobby Johanson
Music Editor . . . . Nic Ratner
Assistant Music Editor. . . . Mick Gormaley
Score Conducted by . . . . . . Blake Neely
Score Recorded and Mixed By
. . . . Alan Meyerson
Orchestrations by . . . . Brad Dechter
Additional Orchestration by
. . . . Chris P. Bacon
Stuart Michael Thomas
Julia Newmann
Auricle Control Systems . . . Richard Grant
Music Preparation by
. . . . Joann Kane Music Service
Music Contractor. . . . . Sandy DeCrescent
Musical Sound Designs. . . . . Clay Duncan
Alex Kharlamov
Mel Wesson
Stuart Michael Thomas
Michael Brooks
Catering By. . . . . TomKats
Unit Publicist . . . . Julie Kuehndorf
Main and End Titles Designed by
. . . . Deborah Ross Film Design
Titles by . . . . Pacific Title
Negative Cutter
. . . . Buena Vista Negative Cutting
Digital Intermediate Facility . . . . . . TDI
Digital Film Colorist
. . . . Stephen Nakamura

"The Thought Of You"
Written by: Edwina Travis-Chin
Provided by: APMmusic

"Midnight Cocktail"
Written by: Stephane Guillaume
Provided by: APMmusic

"Candence Kickoff"
Written by Bert Ferntheil
Provided by APM Music

Financing provided by . . . . Bank of Ireland
International Sales and Distribution by
. . . . Summit Entertainment
Prints by . . . . Technicolor®

Color by . . . . Kodak/Fuji
Chapman Camera Dollies provided by
. . . . . . That Cat Camera Support LLC
The Major League Baseball Trademarks
depicted in this motion picture were licensed
by . . Major League Baseball Properties, Inc.
George Clooney's Wardrobe provided by
. . . . Canali
Watches provided by
. . . . Jaeger-LeCoultre Watches
Clifford Ross photography licensed by
. . . . Sonnebrand Gallery, NYC
Photography licensed by the artist
. . . . Jeffrey Rothstein
Fantasy artwork licensed by the artist
. . . . Steve Roberts

American Humane Association monitored
the animal action.
No animal was harmed in the making of this
film.
(AHA 01205)

The filmmakers wish to extend their personal
thanks to the following for their contribution
to the making of this movie:

Dewey Ballantine Morrison Cohen, LLP
Oaktree Capital Management
Davis Polk & Wardwell
Simpson Thatcher & Bartlett LLP
Weil, Gothsal & Manges
Salisbury Mills Volunteer Fire Department
Cornwall Police Department
Blooming Grove Police Department
Independence Fire Company of Blooming
Grove
Upper Brookville Police Department
Town of Upper Brookville
Town of Monroe
Town of Clarkstown
Town of Cornwall
Community of Worley Heights
Palisades Park Commission
WISN

New York Mayor's Office of Film,
Theatre and Broadcast
City of New York
The Empire State Film Production
"Made In NY" Incentive Program
Mercedes Benz
Datacard
Equity Management
Steve & Jean Geiger
Jerry Huffman, Wisconsin Department of
Tourism
City of Council Bluffs, Iowa
Dick Mattox & James Bane,
Iowa Department of Transportation
The New York State Governor's Office
For Motion Picture and Television
Development

Filmed with PANAVISION®
Cameras and Lenses

MPAA #43163 (logo)

This motion picture © 2007
Clayton Productions, LLC

About the Screenwriter/Director

Tony Gilroy makes his directorial debut with *Michael Clayton*. An acclaimed screenwriter, Tony Gilroy has written several highly successful films, including the international blockbusters *The Bourne Identity, The Bourne Supremacy,* and *The Bourne Ultimatum,* all starring Matt Damon in the role of Jason Bourne.

Gilroy has also written three films for director Taylor Hackford: *Dolores Claiborne,* based on the novel by Stephen King and starring Kathy Bates and Jennifer Jason Leigh; *The Devil's Advocate,* starring Keanu Reeves, Al Pacino, and Charlize Theron; and *Proof of Life,* starring Russell Crowe and Meg Ryan, which Gilroy also executive produced.

Gilroy has also written or co-written *The Cutting Edge,* starring D. B. Sweeney and Moira Kelly; *For Better and for Worse,* starring Patrick Dempsey and Kelly Lynch; *Exreme Measures,* starring Gene Hackman, Hugh Grant, and Sarah Jessica Parker, and directed by Michael Apted; *Bait,* starring Jamie Foxx and directed by Antoine Fuqua; and *Armageddon,* the blockbuster starring Bruce Willis, Ben Affleck, and Billy Bob Thornton, and directed by Michael Bay.

Raised in upstate New York, Gilroy is the son of Pulitzer Prize–winning playwright and filmmaker Frank D. Gilroy. His brother Dan Gilroy is a screenwriter. His brother John Gilroy is a film editor, whose credits include *Michael Clayton.*